THE LEOPARDS
OF LONDOLOZI

THE LEOPARDS
OF LONDOLOZI
—
LEX HES

STRUIK WINCHESTER

Dedicated to the memory of my mother, Esther.

STRUIK
WINCHESTER

An imprint of Struik Publishers (Pty) Ltd
(a member of The Struik Publishing Group (Pty) Ltd)
Cornelis Struik House, 80 McKenzie Street
Cape Town, 8001

Reg. No. 54/00965/07

First published 1991
Second impression 1992
Third impression 1995
Fourth impression 1996

Edited by Phillida Simons
Designed by Jenny Camons
Londolozi map (page 164): Tobie Beele; inset by Dave Snook
World distribution map (page 165): Dave Snook

DTP conversion by BellSet, Cape Town
Colour separations by Chroma Graphics (Overseas) (Pte) Ltd, Singapore
Printed and bound by South China Printing Co. (Pte) Ltd, Hong Kong

ISBN 0 947430 24 5 (Sponsors' Edition)
ISBN 0 947430 23 7 (Collectors' Edition)
ISBN 0 947430 22 9 (Standard Edition)

HALF TITLE PAGE: *A young male leopard peers at an unwary herd of impala.*
TITLE PAGE: *Even while resting during a hunt, an adult female leopard remains on the alert for potential prey.*
ABOVE: *Backlit by the afternoon sun, a leopard strolls through summer grasses.*

CONTENTS

ABOVE: *A pair of young leopards play-fight while their mother is away hunting
in the cool of early morning.*
OVERLEAF: *An adult female and her cub relax between feeds on a lichen-covered granite boulder.*

ACKNOWLEDGEMENTS

I have had the privilege of living and working at Londolozi Game Reserve for the past 15 years or so and I am especially indebted to the owners of the reserve, John and Dave Varty, for imparting their enthusiasm and passion for wildlife. Their youthful spirit, particularly during the early years, was a great inspiration to me.

Over the years, the staff at Londolozi have provided me with a great deal of moral and physical support and I am most grateful to all those people with whom I have worked. I shared many special moments with my fellow rangers and, in particular, I would like to mention Tony and Dérell Adams, John Dixon, Peter le Roux, Ronnie McKelvey, Ian Thomas and James Marshall, participants in many stimulating campfire discussions.

Without the trackers most of these leopard observations wouldn't have been possible. My thanks go to Carlson Mathebula, the late Keys Mathebula, Elmon Mhlongo, Kimbian Mnisi, Judas Ndlovo, and Richard Siwelo, for originally 'finding' the leopards and for sharing knowledge that can't be learned from any book.

In addition I would like to express my gratitude to: Tony Adams, Andrew Lewis and Trevor Lindegger who helped to keep records of the leopards during my absence; Jeremy Anderson, Anthony Bannister, Peter Johnson, Gus Mills, Peter Pickford, David Steele, Duncan Butchart and Leigh Voigt, all of whom gave of their expertise; Dr Roy Bengis, State Veterinarian in the Kruger National Park, who enlightened me on oestrus cycles and on disease; Peter Bester of Fotoquip; Neil Hulett who provided me with photographs of leopards taken in the early days; my wife Lynn; Paddy Hagelthorn; Shan Varty; Norman Mann whose photograph confirmed the sighting of 'our' young male on Sabi-Sabi; Waynne McLintock who kindly set aside time to fly me over Londolozi for aerial photography, and Tedd Schorman for helping me acquire equipment.

A special word of thanks must go to my aunt, Mrs J.C. von Freytag Drabbe and my father Jimmy, for helping to arrange the processing of my favourite film. Without their help, I doubt if we would have achieved the same results.

When I was younger, the photography of Anthony Bannister, Peter Johnson, John Shaw and Hugo von Lawick provided me with endless inspiration and gave me something to which I could aspire.

Finally, a word of appreciation to Phillida Simons and all the staff at Struik involved in the production of the book, including Peter Borchert, Jenny Camons for her sensitivity in the design, and especially Eve Gracie for co-ordinating the project.

LEFT: *As a three-month-old leopard cub peers from behind the trunk of a weeping wattle tree, its expression is a mix of curiosity and concern. Even at this age, the cubs are abandoned for days at a time while the mother hunts.*

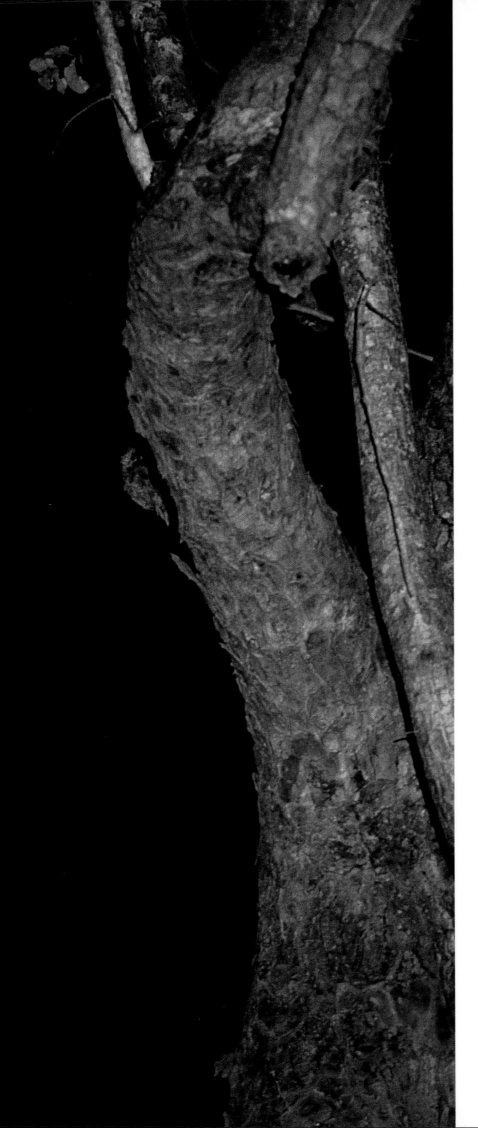

AUTHOR'S NOTE

When we started to obtain regular sightings of the leopards in 1979, I began recording our observations in a notebook in the hope that we would be able to gather sufficient information to reveal more of the leopard's secretive ways. Little did we know that those initial observations would lead to a relationship that has lasted more than a decade and has filled my filing cabinet.

I have based *The Leopards of Londolozi* on these daily records. Everything described in the book has been faithfully reported and is, as far as possible, in chronological order. Important incidents that occurred while I was away were described to me by rangers and trackers. In order to maintain interest I have tended to dwell on the more exciting episodes in the leopards' lives. While all facts, dates and statistics are accurate and I hope that the reader is able to glean a great deal of knowledge about these wonderful animals, the book does not aspire to be a scientific treatise.

Virtually all the observations were made and the photographs taken during the course of conducting daily game drives with visitors. I carried my photographic equipment on the seat alongside me everywhere we went. While I believe the choice of photographic equipment is far less important than the way the photograph is taken, some readers may be interested to know what equipment was used. All photographs were taken using Minolta SRT and XGM cameras with 28 mm, 50 mm, 80–200 mm and 500 mm lenses, and Nikon FM2 cameras with 24 mm, 55 mm, 105 mm, 180 mm and 300 mm lenses. I used powerful Sunpak and Metz flashguns at night.

For wildlife photography, the importance of keeping the camera steady cannot be overemphasized, and I always carry a beanbag which I rest on the dashboard of the Land Rover to support the camera. It is as good as a tripod, far less cumbersome and is probably my most important piece of equipment.

My film of choice is Kodachrome 64 for I value its fine grain and excellent colour balance.

I believe that the task of a wildlife photographer is to convey as much information as possible about his subject through his photographs. The picture shouldn't be simply a record of the animal but should reveal information about its habitat, habits and character. Above all, the beauty and wonder of nature should be communicated to the viewer. I sincerely hope that I have achieved some of this in this collection of photographs.

Lex Hes
Londolozi
March 1991

With graceful ease, a leopard leaps from branch to branch.
Using their tails for balance and retractile claws for gripping, leopards
are completely at home in even the highest trees.

THE BEGINNING

All four wheels of the Land Rover bit into the sand as we moved slowly forward along the dry riverbed. Carlson, my Shangaan tracker, sat on the bonnet scanning the ground in front while, behind me, six guests peered eagerly into the dense riverine vegetation on either side. Tense with anticipation, we passed beneath huge dark-barked jackal-berry trees, yellow-skinned figs and dense thickets of *Rhus* and *Maytenus*. A francolin exploded out of the bush next to the Land Rover, startling us. Above, a flock of redbilled helmetshrikes flitted across the tree canopy.

Suddenly, Carlson's hand went up. 'Ingwe,' he whispered, pointing to a small symmetrical pug-mark in the thick sand. I stopped the Land Rover and, taking my rifle, jumped out of the vehicle to join him as he began to follow the tracks. In the thick sand they were easy to see, their small size indicating that they were the footprints of a female. Carlson showed me where moisture underlying the sand had been exposed by the leopard's passing. So the tracks were fresh!

In the open sand we could follow quickly, but then, abruptly, the tracks swung northwards out of the riverbed. Now the going became more difficult. The ground was harder and the grass thicker but Carlson knew what to look for. Using a combination of skill, keen eyesight, anticipation and luck, he stayed on the tracks. Sometimes a freshly bent grass-stalk provided a clue; sometimes there was a claw-mark in a tree trunk. Once Carlson showed me a single pale-coloured hair caught on a thorn. Every so often a soft patch of sand would reveal a fresh pug-mark, confirming Carlson's conjecture.

Cautiously we moved on along the bank of a gully, Carlson picking out the tracks while I scanned the thicket ahead. A small game path led us down into a dip; on either side of it the dense bush was eerily silent. Suddenly, hardly 10 metres away, we saw the leopard. She was half-crouching in the side path, large yellow eyes glaring fixedly at us, lips bared in a half-snarl as three little bundles of fur disappeared into the bush behind her. Tense and breathless, we slowly backed away, conscious that those cold yellow eyes were following our every move.

With hearts throbbing, we returned to the Land Rover and I started the engine. Without difficulty, I found a route through the bush to the edge of the gully where we had seen the leopard and carefully manoeuvred the vehicle until we were overlooking a pile of granite boulders. There, at their base, was the leopard and, staring at us from behind her, with a mixture of fear and curiosity in their eyes, were three little cubs, not more than two months old.

Quietly, we sat and watched as the leopards began to relax. The cubs, their curiosity satisfied, settled down to suckle but the mother glared at us every now and then until she too began to relax, slowly and efficiently licking her offspring as they took their nourishment. We remained watching for the next half hour as the cubs, their bellies full, tottered unsteadily after one another, tumbling up and down the boulders, pouncing on the mother's tail and clambering up small trees. As we gazed with wonder at a sight so seldom witnessed before, my thoughts turned back to my first years at Londolozi and to the time when the elusive leopard was hardly ever seen...

■ ■ ■

Londolozi is ideal leopard country. It consists of 13 000 hectares of dense woodland patterned with a mosaic of open spaces and provides habitats for a variety of wild animals. The whole area is criss-crossed by dongas – dry riverbeds with sandy bottoms and dense thickets on their banks. Each donga has an identity of its own: Tamboti Donga has a grove of evenly spaced tamboti trees, while Princess Alice Donga is dark, forbidding and completely

Portrait of a leopard with her two-month-old cub as they rest in winter grasses. Prior to 1979, sights like this were unknown at Londolozi. Although we knew the leopards were there, we seldom glimpsed these elusive animals.

overgrown with dense vegetation. The Tugwaan is long, winding and deep, rocky in parts and sandy in others; and then there are the smaller dongas like Three-streaked Donga, Warthog Skull Donga and the Nyatini. Most are tributaries of the Mshabene, a winding wide band of thick sand lined with dense riverine vegetation and the major donga running through the centre of Londolozi. Large jackal-berry trees, sausage trees and mahoganies on the banks provide ideal places for

Trio of Burchell's zebra grazing.

the various antelope and smaller animal species, included lion, hyaena and buffalo, all of them plentiful and relatively easy to see.

To find the game, John and Dave took advantage of the remarkable talents of the local tribal people, the Shangaans. From their fathers and grandfathers they had acquired a knowledge of the bush and, in particular, a skill in tracking which had become legendary. Once they had used these abilities to make a living,

leopards to store their kills while dense thickets of spike-thorn, *Rhus* and long rank grass make perfect cover for hunting. The woodlands alongside the dongas are scattered with numerous termite mounds which, riddled with antbear holes and covered with dense thickets of vegetation, are ideal hiding places for leopard cubs. Scattered throughout the bush are numerous man-made waterholes: Circuit Road Pan, Rhino Dam, Cheetah Pools, Big Dam – all important drinking points built of necessity to ensure a ready supply of water in times of drought. And providing access to the area is a network of jeep tracks, all named after people, places or objects: Tu-tone's Road is called after one of the early Shangaan trackers in the area, and then there are Sunset Bend Road, Inky Thomas's Road, Tortoise Road and others.

This variety of habitats is home to many kinds of wild animals. Grazing species, such as wildebeest, zebra, buffalo, white rhinoceros and warthog, are found in the open areas, while leaf-eaters, such as kudu, giraffe, duiker, steenbuck, bushbuck and nyala, as well as the ubiquitous impala, inhabit the woodlands and the thickets along the dongas. Here, too, are found many other smaller species such as the mongoose, genets, civets, squirrels, porcupine and as many as 300 different bird species.

The northern boundary of Londolozi is the beautiful, perennial Sand River, its many sandbanks covered in reed-beds and palms and its fringes lined with large riverine trees. It is here, on the southern bank of the river, nestling beneath shady jackal-berry and tamboti trees, that the Londolozi camp is situated. And it is here that thousands of local and overseas visitors come each year to see and photograph the wonderful diversity of wild animals. The guests are taken on drives in open Land Rovers by guides who have an affinity with nature and who are able to expose them to Africa in many of its moods. To the visitors, this is always an exciting, emotional and educational experience.

It was to this paradise that I first came in 1976. I joined a group of young people, all of whom had one thing in common: a great love of the natural environment. Two members of the group, John and Dave Varty, were the owners of Londolozi. Not only were these two young men enthusiastic, but they shared passionate dreams for the future of wildlife and for Londolozi in particular – dreams that most people at that time believed would never be realized. Using battered old Land Rovers, John and Dave personally took their visitors out to view the game which, besides

either directly by hunting or trapping wild animals, or indirectly in the employment of hunters. Winnis Mathebula, for example, worked as a tracker for Colonel James Stevenson-Hamilton, first curator of the Kruger National Park, in the early 1900s and later for John and Dave's grandfather. His was an exciting life – he was gored by a buffalo on one occasion and bitten by a black mamba on another – and yet he died at the ripe old age of 85. Another tracker, Tu-tone Sithole, was a very successful poacher before turning his craft to legal use when he started working at Londolozi. Today Londolozi employs young men like Elmon Mhlongo and Kimbian Mnisi who still make a successful living out of their skills but no longer see wild animals as their forefathers did. In the old days, men like Winnis and Tu-tone regarded game either as a source of food or as dangerous predators which were capable of killing men and cattle.

Elmon tells a tale of the days when he was a little boy living close to what is now the southern section of Londolozi. He and his brothers and friends regularly wandered about in the bush, setting snares for small game and hunting down impala with the help of their dogs. One day, during such an outing, Elmon's dogs began to chase something ahead of them and, yapping excitedly, disappeared into dense thickets beside a deep riverbed. Thinking they had cornered an impala, Elmon and his brothers followed the dogs only to discover that they had treed two small leopard cubs. Aware that leopards had killed their father's goats in the past, the boys picked up rocks and stones and pelted the helpless cubs until they fell dead to the ground. Today things have changed and Elmon sees leopards in a completely different perspective. To him, they have become animals for which people are willing to pay to see. He knows that now they are more valuable alive than dead.

Together, John, Dave and the Shangaans developed a technique of finding the animals for their visitors. The tracker would sit on the bonnet of the Land Rover and carefully scan the ground in front of the vehicle for tracks of big game. Once they were found, the tracker would follow on foot accompanied by John or Dave armed with a high-powered rifle. Using their ancient inbred intuition, an incredible amount of patience and amazing perseverance and determination, the trackers would locate the animals and then guide the Land Rover to a position which gave their guests the best viewing possible. At night, the tracker would sit on the back of the Land Rover and he and one of the guests, each manning a spotlight, would scan the bush for the tell-tale glow of eyes. With the aid of these techniques, lion, elephant, rhino and a variety of other animals were regularly seen, much to the delight and excitement of the guests.

The other large predators, cheetah and leopard, were seldom observed, the former because they were so few in number, and the latter because of

Redbilled oxpeckers perch on a Cape buffalo.

their shy elusive nature. Of course, we had always known that there were leopards at Londolozi. We could hear them calling at night; we saw their tracks in the morning and we often found the remains of their kills in trees. Occasionally, we even caught a glimpse of a spotted shape disappearing into the shadowy bush. We knew, too, of biologists who had spent years studying leopards without ever seeing a single animal and were therefore obliged to base their research on radio-telemetry and the analysis of faeces. We could understand why. Gradually, for us, the leopard began to take on a mystical quality.

Always there but never seen, it moved like a ghost in the night, making its kills, leaving its drag-marks and footprints and calling hauntingly into the darkness. Attempts at tracking yielded nothing but pug-marks and occasionally the remains of a carcass abandoned by the leopard long before our arrival. Sometimes, when we found a fresh kill, we would wait for an hour or longer in the hope that the leopard would return. If we left the site and returned 15 minutes later, we would invariably find that the leopard had been back and dragged away the carcass. Typical leopard, we thought. Little did we know then that this mysterious creature would eventually become part of a most intimate relationship between man and wild animal.

Things changed at Londolozi in 1979 while I was away on a trip to the sub-Antarctic. Kimbian Mnisi and another young man, Ken Maggs, had developed a close working relationship, Kimbian imparting to Ken his wealth of Third World knowledge and Ken in turn exposing Kimbian to his own Western values and learning. Working closely together, these two derived great pleasure from following the game, Kimbian doing the actual tracking, and Ken providing security in the form of watchful eyes and a loaded rifle. They would spend hours in their spare time tracking various species of game, often braving considerable danger, and they also devoted time to the search of the mysterious leopard. It was not long before their wonderful enthusiasm was rewarded.

As so often happens, the new development in events started with a little bit of luck. One night, on the off chance of actually seeing a leopard, Ken decided to take his guests on a drive along the Mshabene to an area where he and Kimbian had earlier seen tracks. They had not gone more than a few hundred metres when Kimbian, who was manning one of the spotlights, suddenly clicked his fingers in excitement. Ken jerked the Land Rover to a halt and peered along the beam of Kimbian's spotlight. There, captured in the circle of light, perched precariously in the topmost branches of a tree, were two small spotted animals. At first Kimbian identified them as genets, small cat-like creatures related to the mongoose that are very common at Londolozi, but Ken thought that they were a little too fat. Eventually the truth dawned on them: they had hit the jackpot at last, for the 'genets' were a pair of leopard cubs.

Trembling with excitement, Ken called in the other Land Rovers on his two-way radio and that night 18 visitors and six rangers and trackers were able to view the little leopard cubs before they eventually tumbled out of the tree and disappeared into a hole in the riverbank. Early the following morning, one of the rangers, Philip Knight, returned to the spot to find tracks of the mother and cubs leading away from the area. He and his tracker followed the footprints until they discovered the cubs in another lair but once again there was no sighting of the mother.

Over the next few weeks the trackers began through skilful tracking to build up a picture of the mother leopard's movements and it gradually became apparent that she would move her cubs to a new lair every few days, presumably as a safety precaution against predators. Using their remarkable skills, the trackers were generally able to locate the new lair whenever the mother made a move. Sometimes they would pick up a track of only the female and, aware that she was afraid of vehicles and people, they would follow the footprints backwards until a large number of cub tracks indicated the situation of the lair. Once it had been found, they could almost guarantee a viewing of the cubs for a few days before the leopard mother made another move.

Initially, she was very shy and there were no sightings of her, but as the weeks went by both rangers and trackers began to catch glimpses of her in the vicinity of the cubs. By stopping the Land Rovers as soon as she was seen and remaining very still, they were able to get longer and longer views of her. She had to return to the cubs regularly to suckle them and this proved a help as the instinct to care for them gradually got the better of her fear of vehicles. By the time the cubs were two months old, rangers and trackers were getting regular views of the mother leopard.

The sensitivity of the rangers played a very important part in this habituation process. Whenever it seemed that the mother leopard was becoming agitated, the Land Rovers backed off and let her be. Within six months, she had completely accepted the presence of the vehicles and this incredible development led to many direct observations of wild leopards that had never before been made. Above all, it led to a relationship between the leopards of Londolozi and its rangers and trackers that has lasted a decade and continues to this day. This book is the story of that remarkable relationship.

ABOVE: *Footprints in the sand, a drag mark and a blood
trail are evidence that a leopard and its kill have passed this way.*
RIGHT: *Date palms, reeds and spike-thorn thickets provide
ideal cover for an adult female leopard hunting along the Sand River.*
OVERLEAF: *Leopards have stunningly beautiful coats. The black spots,
scattered in rosettes over the back and flanks, give way to single spots on the head,
neck and limbs.*

LEFT: *Early morning mist is characteristic of the autumn months of April and May.*
ABOVE: *Raising a shower of spray, a hippopotamus surfaces for air with only his nostrils protruding as the sunlight shimmers on the water's surface.*

Early on a winter morning, an old elephant bull emerges from the mist-enshrouded bush to amble across a clearing. Until recently, the only elephants seen regularly at Londolozi were single nomadic bulls such as this one, but now a small breeding group has established itself from a group of young elephants introduced in the mid-seventies.

Once restricted to a few suitable localities along the Sand River, waterbuck are now widespread and common. They
live in small groups, usually comprising six to 12 females and young. The young males form separate bachelor herds
while adult males play a territorial role. Waterbuck, as their name indicates, are always found close to surface water.

STICKNYAWO

As the months went by, the mother leopard's pattern of behaviour became clearer. When the cubs were very young, she would leave them in a safe place such as a termite mound in which there were holes covered by vegetation, under dense piles of dead brush or in natural crevices formed by piles of granite boulders. Then she would go hunting, returning every few hours to suckle the cubs. As they grew a little older, the mother would spend slightly longer periods away from the lair, returning only when she had made a kill and then leading the cubs to the kill site. Once they had consumed the meat, the mother would take the cubs to a new lair before setting off on her next hunt.

It was most rewarding for rangers, trackers and guests to find the cubs on their own at the lair site. The rangers would drive the Land Rovers to within a few metres of the spot, switch off engines and wait. Within a few minutes an inquisitive spotted face would poke out of a hole, to be followed a moment later by another. The two cubs would then clamber clumsily over fallen logs, climb small saplings, fall out of trees, and then run around after one another, catching each other's tails, play-fighting and stalking rustles in the grass. They were an endless source of amusement and the smaller cub, especially, began to endear herself to everyone. Often she would stop her play, cock an enquiring eye at the Land Rover and then slowly stalk it until she was less than a metre away. Then suddenly she would leap up and scamper after her sister again. It seemed almost as though she had two playmates, her sister and the Land Rover.

The cubs were about three months old when Elmon made an important discovery. He and Philip Knight were tracking them on foot along a game trail near the Dudley-Sparta Vlei, a non-perennial reed-covered marsh in the east of Londolozi, when he realized that there was something unusual about the tracks. He kept finding a slight drag-mark where a footprint should have been. His observation was confirmed when the tracks went through a patch of soft sand which made the drag-mark clearer. It appeared to Elmon that one of the leopards was dragging a foot on the ground and if this were so, the cub would probably be at a distinct disadvantage. Naturally, Elmon and Philip hoped that the injury was temporary.

When they came upon the leopards at the vlei, they noticed immediately that the smaller cub was limping very badly, swinging her hip awkwardly from one side to the other in order to accommodate the bad leg and showing a good deal of discomfort as she walked. With the aid of binoculars, Philip could see that the little leopard's right hind leg was badly misshapen. To him the scene was totally incongruous. Here was one of the most beautiful animals in Africa moving about in complete freedom but marred by a horrible disfigurement.

Distressed at their discovery, the two men wondered how the unfortunate little cub could have suffered such mutilation. Then, as they watched the leopards at play, they realized how an accident could have occurred. One of the cubs tried clumsily to climb up a tree by scrambling along a branch that could barely hold her weight. Near the top of the tree, the branch snapped and the cub came tumbling down, catching her leg in a fork as she fell and so halting her descent. She hung there briefly, her full weight on the trapped leg, and then managed to wriggle free and drop to the ground. It seemed quite possible to Philip and Elmon that the little leopard could have torn and twisted the ligaments in her leg in this way and so caused what appeared to be a permanent injury.

Over the next few months, we all watched the little lame leopard with concern. How long, we wondered, would she survive? Would she ever be able to hunt for herself? Was she able to climb trees successfully? How would she stand up to another

Portrait of Sticknyawo. Each leopard has its own unique spot-pattern. Small groups of usually two or three spots, which vary in size and spacing from one leopard to another, cluster above the point where the whiskers grow from the face. These spots form the basis of our identification system.

leopard in a fight and how could she escape predators? These were questions that could be answered only by keeping a close watch on her, and to everyone at Londolozi the survival prospects of the little lame cub seemed very bleak. Meanwhile, we grew more and more attached to her and it was not long before the trackers had given her a name – 'Sticknyawo'. The word was a curious fusion of English and African in which 'stick', as in walking stick, was combined with 'nyawo', the Zulu for leg or foot. Thus its literal translation was 'Peg leg'.

Whitefaced owl feeding on a rodent.

One question that constantly recurs at Londolozi concerns the naming of leopards. It is in man's nature to apply human emotions and feelings to the animals around him and one of the natural extensions of this is to give them names. Perhaps by doing so we feel that we have some sort of control over them and certainly it does help us to identify individuals. Nevertheless, at Londolozi there is a general feeling that by naming the animals we detract from the true wildness of the place, part of a wildness that is fast disappearing all over the world. So, in giving Sticknyawo a name, we were making an exception and breaking from our accepted custom.

■ ■ ■

By the time I got back to Londolozi from the sub-Antarctic in 1980, the mother and her two cubs had become completely habituated to the presence of the Land Rovers. Previously I had only caught glimpses of spotted shapes disappearing into the darkness, so my first view of the cubs one afternoon soon after my return seemed quite unbelievable. They were lying in the open near an island of bush in the middle of Gert's Clearing close to the Dudley-Sparta Vlei, seemingly totally oblivious of the Land Rovers parked only a few metres away. What I had seen earlier had given me no hint whatsoever of the remarkable beauty of these animals. Their spotted coats were stunning: golden yellow on the back and flanks merged gradually with soft pure white fur on the belly. Over the entire coat there was a scattering of black spots, those on the flanks and back forming circular clumps or rosettes as if someone, with finger-tips held together, had dabbed paint on to the fur. Somehow this astonishing coloration blended perfectly with the natural surroundings, making the leopard one of the most difficult animals to spot. The cubs' tails, which they regularly and casually flicked across their bodies to keep the flies at bay, seemed to have a life of their own; long and snake-like, they were covered in spots right up to their pure white, twitching tips. But most startling of all were the leopards' eyes: large, pale yellow, ice cold, they glared at us from spotted faces with an expression that warned: 'Don't mess with me'.

Both cubs were females, but it seemed that they had already developed individual characters. Sticknyawo was slightly smaller than her sister and far more relaxed with the Land Rovers. She was very inquisitive and not afraid to come up to the vehicle to peer quizzically up at the people sitting in it, or to walk casually past, not more than a metre away. Her sister was much more reclusive, keeping her distance and not showing the same curiosity.

I could not have asked for a better sighting of the two cubs. They were waiting for the mother to return from a hunt and had ventured out of the thicket where she had left them to get a better view of their surroundings. The afternoon sun was shining on them and their coats gleamed in the warm light as I watched in awe while they played with each other like two large domestic kittens. Sticknyawo stalked up to a small branch that was moving gently in the breeze, pounced on it and shook it vigorously as though she were making a kill. As she settled down to chew on it, her sister, watching her intently, crouched low and began to crawl slowly and carefully towards her, placing her feet silently one in front of the other. Every time Sticknyawo looked up, her sister froze, waiting for the smaller cub to drop her head before resuming her stalk. When the sister cub was no more than a metre away, she gathered her legs together and suddenly leapt at Sticknyawo, landing on top of her. Sticknyawo responded by biting her sister gently on the neck and holding on to her with her forepaws, before scampering around a bush with her sister on her tail. And so the game continued, the cubs, with seemingly unlimited energy, running around after each other and apparently quite oblivious of the presence of the Land Rovers.

It became obvious from the games the leopards were playing that Sticknyawo was more than holding her own. She was able to move just as quickly as her sister by raising the gammy leg off the ground and running on the other three and when we saw how she scampered up and down and through the branches of the trees any doubts that we may have had about her climbing abilities were completely dispelled. Even in play-fighting, a kind of simulation of the real thing during which leopards rise up on their hind legs and bite and cuff one another with their forepaws, Sticknyawo gave as good as she got. But, to begin with, these were just games, and we still did not know how she would eventually cope with life on her own when agility and quick reaction would be all-important. It did not seem as though three legs would be enough to catch a speeding, jinking impala, or to avoid the swift danger of a threatening lioness.

As the cubs grew older, the mother spent progressively longer periods away from them and as a result they would spend three or four days at a time, sometimes longer, patiently waiting for her to return. They began to wander further from the place where their mother had left them as their curiosity led them after a variety of interesting sights and sounds. The slightest rustle in the grass and Sticknyawo would jump up and cautiously stalk, eventually pouncing too late to catch the perpetrator, be it a mongoose, bird or some other small animal. Sometimes the cubs would come across impala or duiker which they, in their amateurish way, would attempt to stalk, but invariably the ever-alert antelope would spot the leopards from a long way off. It became apparent to us that these were not just games but that the cubs were actually learning the skills needed for their future survival. Everything, from the

Northern mottled toad croaking.

playful stalk after a rustle in the grass to their quick chase and pounce games, would eventually develop into a life-and-death hunt. They seemed to be learning by experience, making errors, trying the stalk again, getting closer, making another mistake, trying yet again and improving all the time.

One night, when the cubs were about 13 months old and spending more time away from each other, Sticknyawo's sister made her first kill – a young scrub hare that she accidentally flushed while stalking a duiker. She picked up the squealing, kicking creature but obviously did not know what to do with it. She walked about with the hare in her mouth, her sharp bites obviously inflicting wounds on the hare but not killing it outright. Every so often she would put the animal down, and when it attempted to run away, she would catch it again without too much difficulty. This cat-and-mouse game continued for at least 15 minutes until eventually the hare died from its wounds and the young leopard settled down to eat it. She obviously still had a lot to learn, but at least she had made her first kill.

Sticknyawo, in the meantime, was not having much luck. We saw her on many occasions hunting various animals, sometimes spending over an hour on the stalk. She seemed to have an endless amount of determination but we never saw her meet with any success. As we observed several more kills made by her sister – a mongoose here, a monkey there – we realized that Sticknyawo was lagging behind and we began to wonder if her injured leg was beginning to tell on her. Fortunately the mother was still providing both cubs with food, and as we had learnt from guide books that leopards do not finally leave their cubs until they are about 22 months old, we felt that Sticknyawo still had a chance of reaching maturity. It was not long before we found out just how wrong the guide books can be.

November brought the first summer rains; within days the well-grazed grass was transformed into a lush green lawn and new shoots began to appear on the hitherto leafless trees. In the middle of the month, about four weeks after Sticknyawo's sister had made her first kill, the mother leopard moved the cubs from an impala kill to a safe area in a donga alongside Tu-tone's Road. She stayed with them during that day and in the evening she set off on her hunt. It was a good area for the leopards – plenty of cover along the donga, large trees for them to climb into when threatened with danger, a woodland on one side, a clearing on

the other and an abundance of game for them to hunt. The impala were beginning to drop their lambs and this provided the cubs with an ideal opportunity to practise their hunting, as the new-born lambs were not as alert or as quick as their parents.

While the mother was away, we visited the cubs daily, not always finding both as they were by this time more or less independent of each other. Sticknyawo's sister, the more adventurous of the two, was now moving further and further afield while Sticknyawo stayed in almost the same spot from day to day. We began to feel anxious about her: she was not showing anything like the spirit that she had revealed when she was younger and she did not seem to have nearly as much energy as her sister of whom, after about a week, we lost track.

We also began to wonder where the mother was for never before had she spent such a long time away from the cubs. With each daily visit, we became more and more despondent. Sticknyawo still had not killed anything for herself and it was by this stage quite obvious that she was losing condition. Her hip bones were beginning to protrude and her coat was losing its lustre. At the end of two weeks, we realized that the mother was not going to return to Sticknyawo. Her work as a parent was now complete and she had gone off to pursue her solitary existence until the arrival of another litter of cubs. Sticknyawo was only 14 months old, fully eight months younger than the guide book's estimated age of independence.

A controversial question cropped up at this time, a question that was to arise again and again as our relationship with the leopards developed. Should we interfere with the natural cycle of events and help Sticknyawo through her crisis? We at Londolozi had a *laissez-faire* policy: nature, we had always felt, should be left to run its course, and this was something in which we still believed. But now things were different. For the first time we had become emotionally involved with a wild animal, and human emotion, as everyone knows, is an enormously powerful force.

Fortunately, we were able to avoid making a decision in this particular case, because one day, nearly a month after the mother had left the cubs, we came across Sticknyawo sitting proudly in the woodland with a large banded mongoose dangling from her mouth. At last she had made her first kill! For almost half an hour she walked around with it in her mouth as though she were showing off. Several times she carried it up into a tree and then carried it down again, until she eventually settled down in the long grass to eat her kill. We were overjoyed. Perhaps it was our imagination, but it seemed that Sticknyawo's coat had already taken on a new shine.

After that we watched her closely and, two days after she had killed the mongoose, we found her feeding on a young impala lamb. Two kills in three days – it seemed that all the barriers had

ABOVE AND LEFT: *A three-month-old leopard cub playfully scrambles up and down the beautifully textured trunk of a tamboti tree and then finds a resting place from which to look down at his mother. This ability to climb trees is vital for the cubs' survival and they are adept at it by the time they are four months old.*
OVERLEAF: *An adult female leopard and her three-month-old cub drink together from a rain-filled pan. Although leopards obtain sufficient moisture from their kills and are not dependent on surface water, they will drink where it is available.*

been broken and that Sticknyawo had success- fully pulled through the first major crisis of her young life. Almost as though the kills had spurred her on, she began to cover greater distances. We saw her less often from then on, but even so, every few days we would find her on a kill or drinking at a waterhole with belly full, or simply resting languidly in the shade of a thicket. Her gammy leg proved to be of great help to the trackers as it served to identify her. She was now roaming over an area of some 600 hectares and looked in superb condition.

During the early months of 1981 we saw very little of the mother leopard. She was on her own now and as she no longer had cubs to anchor her to specific areas she was moving much further afield. However, we did come across her every now and again and it was pleasing to observe that she still had very little

Large-spotted genet.

fear of the Land Rovers. We began to wonder when she would produce another litter and whether we would be privileged to see her new cubs. There was very little information on this subject in the guide books so we had no idea of when to expect such an exciting event. All we could do was watch and wait.

It was at about this time that the unique character of our leopard-viewing was brought home to us as we began to receive telephone calls and letters enquiring about the leopards' pro- gress from guests who had seen them. Many of them returned again and again and the word very quickly spread that there were leopards to be seen at Londolozi Game Reserve. People who had been visiting the Kruger National Park regularly for 15 years or more without ever coming across a single leopard, jumped at the opportunity when they heard that they were to be seen at Londolozi. Amazingly, within the brief space of three days, we were able to give them perfect sightings of the leopards that were now becoming so familiar.

Among these guests was the Hulett family – Neil, Morag and their three children – all of them wildlife enthusiasts who had been visiting the Kruger National Park for a number of years. They always seemed to have a good deal of luck there yet never once had they seen a leopard. As soon as they heard about Londolozi, they made a booking and were rewarded with leopard views on their very first visit. They loved Londolozi and from then on returned two or three times every year.

Late one afternoon in May 1981 Dave Varty was taking the Huletts around Londolozi when he came across the footprints of a male and female leopard on Sunset Bend Road near an area of dense vegetation called Princess Alice Bush. Dave and his tracker got out of the vehicle and investigated the tracks which seemed to be heading off into a thicket alongside the road. Suddenly a low growling was heard from within the thicket. Dave and his tracker froze in their tracks and then backed slowly in the direction of the Land Rover, the growling all the while increasing in intensity. Everyone in the party expected a leopard

to burst out of the bush at any second, but nothing appeared. Instead, the growling in- creased steadily, reaching a climax with a sud- den loud burst of sound. Nobody present, not even Dave, had ever heard anything like it.

By this time it was growing dark, so the spotlights were taken out as Dave tried to ma- noeuvre the Land Rover towards the source of the sound. Then suddenly Neil saw two sets of eyes glowing in the dark and immediately sig- nalled Dave to stop. In a little clearing in the thicket there was a pair of leopards, one much larger than the other – obviously a male and a female. Neil, who had a video camera with him, began to film them when suddenly, through his viewing screen, he saw the smaller leopard get up, brush past the male twice and then settle down immediately in front of him in a crouching position, giving the low growl that we had heard earlier. Then the male stood up and mounted her and, as the mating progressed, the growling of both leopards intensified. Then the male bit the female gently on the neck; suddenly there was the loud burst of sound that had been heard earlier and the male leapt off the female to avoid being cuffed by her. It was an incredible sight and in Neil's excitement he had not registered that he had been filming the whole process.

This was the first occasion, as far as we knew, that anyone had ever witnessed the mating of leopards in the wild. It was very similar to the mating of lions, a process which the female initiates by seductively rubbing her body against the male several times before settling down into a crouching position. There was the same biting of the neck by the male and a similar growling followed by the aggressive reaction of the female. However, there was one difference: whereas the lions seemed to make a public display of pairing, usually in open areas, the leopards kept the whole process extremely private, choosing for it the densest bush they could find. We were unaware of it at the time, but we later discovered that the female involved in this particular mating was the mother of Sticknyawo and her sister.

We were now moving into the dry winter months and Londolozi began to wear its drab winter coat. The long grass had turned brown, the leafless trees took on a stark lifeless appear- ance and the bitingly cold night air contrasted strongly with the pleasant warmth of the clear, sunny days. As the waterholes dried up, the game began concentrating around the few remaining, in this way making viewing easier. With the reduced foliage and the collapsing grass stalks, visibility improved and we began to get more and more regular sightings of Sticknyawo.

Occasionally she provided the trackers with some hair-raising experiences – experiences which served to convince us of the passive nature of this remarkable leopard. One day in June, while Elmon and Philip were tracking her in the Tamboti Donga area, Elmon somehow became separated from Philip which meant that he no longer had the protection of a loaded rifle behind him. Such was his determination, however, that he continued tracking, comforting himself with the knowledge that at least he had a small penknife in his pocket. The tracks led him into a stand of scented thorn so dense that it was almost impenetrable. Unarmed within a thick wall of bush in which a leopard was lurking, Elmon knew just how dangerous his situation was. Nevertheless, he continued following the tracks until he detected in the grass a fresh drag-mark, indicating the spot where some animal had been killed. Elmon took the knife out of his pocket and, moving cautiously, was following the drag when he heard a twig crack close behind his right foot. He swung around, knife at the ready. There, less than a metre away, crouched in the grass and staring up at him, was Sticknyawo. Her face showed no sign of aggression and, as Elmon remained

Pied kingfisher and darter.

rooted to the spot, she casually stood up, took a step closer and picked up a young impala that she had killed. With the kill in her mouth, she looked at Elmon for a moment, then turned her back on him and sauntered off into the woodland, dragging her booty with her.

We were to learn, while tracking leopards on foot over the next few years, that this behaviour is typical of the animals. If leopards sense the approach of a human, they tend to lie low watching the person as he, oblivious of the animal's presence, walks past. However, as we were to discover, if the human chanced to see the leopard lying low, it will immediately charge. But in this, Sticknyawo was different. Once discovered, she would usually stand up as if to say, 'Okay, you've seen me. Now let me get on with my business.' Then she would just walk away, displaying no aggression whatsoever.

Shortly after the meeting with Elmon, Sticknyawo had another encounter that actually put her life in jeopardy. A wounded leopard is considered to be highly dangerous and the sight of one is usually enough for a man to reach for his rifle to protect himself and anyone else who might come across the luckless animal. A temporary warden working on a property bordering on Londolozi found himself in just such a situation. He was walking along the boundary when he suddenly came across Sticknyawo standing in the road. On seeing him, she slowly limped off into Londolozi and the warden, thinking that he had found a dangerous wounded leopard, ran back to his vehicle to fetch his rifle. He searched the area intensively but, fortunately for Sticknyawo, without success. That afternoon, we received an agitated telephone call from him warning us that there was a wounded leopard on our property but, after hearing his description, we were able to reassure him that all was well and that Sticknyawo was well known to us.

While this story ended happily, it did point to one of the risks that Sticknyawo faced: the chance that she could wander on to a neighbouring property and be shot legally by hunters eager to

bag a trophy and her relative fearlessness of humans made her particularly vulnerable. We decided to write to the neighbours enclosing photographs of Sticknyawo and explaining her story in the hopes that their goodwill would ensure her protection. We like to think that this precaution was successful.

During this time, our sightings of the mother leopard were few and far between. At one stage, a whole month passed without our seeing her, and we began to feel anxious about her fate. Then, one afternoon in early August 1981, we came across a pair of leopards at Big Dam on the bank of the Mshabene in the heart of Londolozi. One, a male, had chased the other, a female, into the top of a marula tree. The male was very shy and ran off when the vehicles approached, but the female stayed in the tree, the afternoon sun shining into her eyes as she looked down at the disappearing male. We realized then that this female was Sticknyawo's mother. She had obviously been involved in a clash of some sort as there was a gash on her nose and a small tear in one ear. Apart from these light injuries, which were later to prove useful in identifying her, the mother leopard looked in good condition.

We watched her and photographed her as she sat among the branches. Then, as the sun dropped towards the horizon, she stretched lazily, yawned, and climbed easily down from the tree, her feet striking the ground noiselessly. As she began moving southwards, she became more difficult to see in the gathering dusk, her body blending perfectly with her surroundings and only the white tail-tip betraying her position. When it became too dark to see her, we connected the spotlights and continued following her, the bright beams probing like feelers into the darkness. She seemed to be moving with purpose in a south-westerly direction, not stopping to listen or watch in the way one would expect from a hunting leopard, but simply walking steadily, only stopping every few metres to scent-mark against a tree trunk or bush.

We wondered why she was moving so purposefully. Possibly, we thought, she had been to Big Dam for a drink and now was on her way back to a kill she had made earlier. After about half an hour most of the other Land Rovers left to view other game, leaving our Land Rover and John Varty's bumping and winding through the darkness as we followed the mother leopard. She continued, wending her way through the night, her glimmering body lit up in the blackness. Every so often we would pick up the glowing eyes of a herd of impala, but the mother leopard ignored them, on her way passing marula and bushwillow trees whose trunks stood ghostly white in the beams of the spotlights.

About an hour after we began following her, she disappeared into a pile of granite boulders very close to Inky Thomas's Road. Thinking that she would emerge on the other side, we drove around to wait for her. We remained there a while and then, as we saw and heard nothing, we decided to return to the spot where she had disappeared. Moving carefully along the edge of the boulders we scanned the crevices until Elmon, who was tracking for me that night, hissed at me to stop. His light was shining into a vertical crevice so narrow that a leopard could barely squeeze through it. Deep inside, we could just make out the form of the mother leopard lying across the opening with no more than a square foot of her skin visible. And, protruding just above the mother's body as they suckled, were the tiny ears of a pair of very small leopard cubs.

Incredible though it seemed, the mother leopard had led us, without any attempt at shaking us off or even so much as a glance over her shoulder, directly to her new-born cubs. More than two years of patient following had finally been rewarded and now we had certain proof that the mother had completely accepted the presence of the Land Rovers. However, we were soon to learn, by means of a number of aggressive encounters, that this tolerance could by no means be taken for granted.

That evening, around the campfire, the animated conversation was about little else but leopards. We guessed the age of the cubs to be less than a week – and then it suddenly dawned on us that we had actually witnessed their conception. The gestation period of leopards is about three-and-a-half months and the pairing that Dave and the Huletts had witnessed had taken place in May. The dates fitted perfectly and the pieces of the leopard puzzle were beginning to fall neatly into place.

We saw the little cubs on two or three occasions at the rocks during the next few days, but then the mother moved them and we were unable to discover where she had gone. The rest of August brought regular sightings of Sticknyawo and the mother, but only one more of the cubs. Unfortunately, the end of August came far too quickly for me, as September meant that I had to leave for another trip to the sub-Antarctic. Reluctantly I bade farewell to Londolozi and the leopards and headed south.

■   ■   ■

In June 1982 when I returned to Londolozi, I was met with the good news that the two little cubs, a male and a female, were now 11 months old and still progressing well, and that Sticknyawo too seemed to be well established in an area to the south-west of the mother's territory. I could not wait to get out into the bush to see the leopards, particularly Sticknyawo, once again. On my first afternoon at the camp, I drove out to the Tugwaan, a large donga to the south of Londolozi where Sticknyawo had been seen a week earlier, but although I searched the area intensively I found nothing.

Early the next morning I was out again, this time with Elmon, and very soon we were fortunate enough to pick up Sticknyawo's familiar tracks near the donga. It proved a long and arduous trail

A leopard cub's first kills, which it makes at about nine months, are usually small animals. Here a young leopard leaps playfully into the air, a scrub hare dangling from its mouth.

as she kept going around in circles through extremely rocky country covered with dense vegetation but at last, thanks largely to Elmon's skills, we found her. She was hunting a herd of impala using large dolomite boulders as cover. After hearing from the other rangers how well she was doing, I found this first sighting of her a great disappointment for she had obviously been involved in a fight. There were fresh wounds below her left eye, on her left cheek and on her neck, and there was a bleeding gash on the inside of her right front leg. It was clear that she had somehow had a clash with one of the other predators – hyaena, lion or possibly even another leopard.

Leopards are territorial, defending their particular areas first of all by means of scent-marking and calling and then, if these signs are ignored, resorting to violent confrontation to evict any intruders. It is evident from our observations that younger leopards are tolerated by other leopards in their territories only until they reach sexual maturity at about two-and-a-half to three years. At this age, the younger leopard has to take life more seriously by observing the 'rules of the game' and avoiding the areas of other more powerful leopards. In order to establish a territory of her own, the younger leopard would have to either find a vacant area, or defeat another leopard in a fight. It seemed that Sticknyawo had reached that stage in her life, as she was now two-and-a-half years old.

Sticknyawo stalked the impala, slinking from rock to rock as she drew closer. Then, suddenly, the impala saw her and gave their alarm calls, explosive snorts that immediately told the leopard that she had been seen. She turned her back on the herd and strolled down to a rock pool and drank. Apart from her wounds, she seemed in good condition, well fed, coat shiny and with a brightness in her eyes. We left Sticknyawo resting in the shade of a *Tecomaria* thicket and returned to camp, wondering how she was going to fare.

A week later, we had another sighting of Sticknyawo, this time near Big Dam, right in the middle of the mother's territory. It was clear to us that this move had been caused by pressure from another leopard to the south-west. But how would the mother react to this intrusion by her daughter? Sticknyawo remained in the Big Dam area for another two weeks, making two or three kills and somehow avoiding contact with the mother until, at the end of June, the two leopards encountered each other. There was a brief aggressive clash at Cheetah Pools, but Sticknyawo managed to avoid serious injury by clambering up to the top of a knob-thorn tree, where, with the advantage of height, she was able to defend herself successfully. The mother eventually left the area, but this seemed to be warning enough for Sticknyawo, for we found her the next morning moving steadily away from the territory in a westerly direction.

Over the next four months, she spent all her time in the area to the south-west, making kills and apparently settling down again while the resident leopard was nowhere evident. But in November, there was a new development.

Sticknyawo began calling, making the repeated grunting sound like the sawing of wood that communicates territorial intent. She had been lucky up to now, but this calling was sure to bring any territorial leopard hurrying in her direction. At this time, she was ranging around a permanent waterhole called Green Pan, so named because of the dense layer of green algae covering the water's surface. Here, on 20 November, she killed a young female impala and then hauled it up into a milkberry tree. It was an ideal position: a vantage point from which she could see the surrounding country with drinking-water only metres away where she had every chance of ambushing any game coming down to drink. Obviously deciding that this would be her territory, she called regularly each night. And still there was no sign of another leopard in the vicinity.

Then, on 25 November, five days after she had killed the impala at Green Pan, we found Sticknyawo lying beside the vehicle track leading to the pan. She had bite-marks on her neck and down her back, her teeth were bared in a half-snarl and in the sand around her there were signs of a struggle. Our hearts sank at the discovery. Sticknyawo was dead.

For us, it was a sad day. We had watched the little lame leopard grow up against all odds from a tiny clumsy two-month-old cub, playing and tumbling and feeding and sleeping with her sister, into a fully-grown female leopard hunting and enduring on her own. For two-and-a-half years we had shared her ups and downs, her struggle to survive when her mother deserted her and her subsequent successes as she began to make regular kills and to establish herself. At long last it had been possible to observe at first hand the intimate habits of a wild leopard. Countless visitors to Londolozi had also become deeply involved with Sticknyawo and had left with a lasting impression of this most beautiful of African cats. Many returned again and again to follow her progress. Now she was no longer with us.

The trackers were able to reconstruct what had happened by studying the signs around the pan. There were tracks showing that Sticknyawo had arrived at the pan from the north, and there were also the tracks of a large male leopard approaching from the south. Almost at the edge of the pan, the tracks met. What happened next was unclear: there was a confusion of tracks, scuff-marks and deeply gouged claw-marks in the soft earth, but it is certain that the result of the confrontation was a protracted fight ending in Sticknyawo's death. Her gammy leg had no doubt affected her speed, balance and agility and had almost certainly put her at a distinct disadvantage.

To this day it remains a mystery why a male leopard should have killed a female, especially one reaching sexual maturity. Possibly, she was coming into oestrus and this had attracted the male. The close physical contact during the pairing could have have led to a fight, for mating is an aggressive affair. Then there was the possibility that the male had perceived Sticknyawo's disability as a sign of weakness and had attacked her. Or, we wondered, could they have fought over a kill? We searched the area intensively, but there was no sign of meat anywhere. We shall probably never know what led to Sticknyawo's death, but no matter what happened she will always be remembered. Green Pan was re-named 'Sticknyawo's Pan' in her honour.

An adult female leopard bunches her legs under her before springing into a marula tree. At Londolozi the ability to climb trees is essential if the leopard is to survive the ever-present threat of lion and spotted hyaena, predators that are more powerful and heavily-built than it is. Confrontation must be avoided at all costs and the leopard's best means of escape is to climb trees.

Autumn at Londolozi can pass by virtually unnoticed. There is a swift turning of foliage from green to soft shades of yellow, orange and brown, colours that last for only a few days before the leaves fall. For those aware of it, the bush has a subtle beauty, as seen in this tapestry of autumn colours in a mixed Combretum/Acacia *woodland.*

Resting on a newly burnt patch of ground, the mother leopard merges into a scattering of fallen brown and orange leaves. The leopard's camouflage is most effective in the winter months when the colours in the coat blend perfectly with the tawny grass and dark shadows. In summer the leopard disappears into the dense green vegetation.

LEFT: *Safely out of reach of predators, a young leopard cub peers down from the higher branches of a leadwood tree.*
ABOVE: *Leopards defend their territories by means of calling and scent-marking, a ritual that begins with the leopard's sniffing a bush or, as here, a fallen tree trunk. It then rubs its face and body against the bush or tree and rounds off the process with a swish of its raised tail and a few squirts of urine.*

THE LION THREAT

During her short life, Sticknyawo had begun to reveal to us many hitherto unknown secrets of the leopard's life history, but there remained many mysteries which we hoped to solve. For example, we had no idea how many leopards there were in the Londolozi area. We wondered how the various leopards related to one another, and especially what relationship existed between males and females for up to that time we had never once had a really good sighting of a male. We wondered, too, how the leopards related to the other predators in the area, particularly to lions – a subject we were to learn much about in the months following Sticknyawo's death. Then there was the question of their hunting techniques, their preferred prey and their feeding methods. All these were questions that we hoped to answer through further observations of the mother and her new litter of cubs.

By July 1982, with the cold bite of winter in the night air and the days pleasantly warm and clear, we had got to know the two leopard cubs intimately. Once again, each leopard seemed to have its own distinct character, the female being far more relaxed with the Land Rovers than the male. It was at this time, when the cubs were 11 months old, that we began to understand the enormous threat that lions pose to leopards.

Early one morning we were following the three leopards through a patch of thick bush near Big Dam, a man-made waterhole built by John and Dave's father around 1965, when the male cub suddenly ran off into a thicket. As we lost sight of him, we heard a scuffle and a loud bleating grunt. Realizing that he had managed to catch something, we raced through the bush to find the young leopard in the process of throttling a young male impala. As far as we knew it was his first kill, and he had accomplished it quite expertly, catching the impala without much trouble and very quickly clamping his mouth over the throat so as to prevent loud bleating that could attract scavengers

such as hyaena and lion. The male cub held on to his victim's throat for what seemed a very long time but gradually the impala's kicking subsided and eventually it stopped breathing. Immediately, the leopard released his hold and, panting heavily, sat up and looked around before moving off to relax in the shade of a large-fruited bushwillow tree. His mother and sister had been watching and, as he moved off, the mother came in and settled down to feed on the kill. Throughout the rest of the day, the three leopards took turns to feed.

The following morning, we found two lionesses hunting in the area close to the leopard's kill. At first we thought that they would bypass the site, but then they suddenly stopped and sniffed the air. Quickly, they turned towards the unmistakable smell, breaking into a run as they got closer. As we approached the thicket where the kill had been made, we saw one leopard cub scampering down from a tree and another bounding off into the woodland, a lioness close on its heels. With our hearts in our throats, we followed as best we could and, after a few minutes of searching, we found all three leopards safely ensconced in the tops of trees with the lions on the ground below. It was a close thing for the leopards. Had they not been so wary and if there had been no convenient trees in the area, one or more of them could have been killed by the lions. The importance of suitable habitat for the leopards' well-being became clear to us. Without dense cover and the safety of large trees in the area, at least one of the leopards would have been doomed.

The last occasion on which we saw the mother with her cubs was at the end of July 1982 when they were about 12 months old. They were still in the vicinity of Big Dam, an area ideal for predator and prey alike. There was drinking-water in the dam; an open clearing surrounding it provided ideal grazing for wildebeest, zebra, impala and warthog, and the dense riverine

A young male lion rests at the end of a long summer day, his face lit by the late afternoon sunshine. Lions at Londolozi are predominantly nocturnal, rising as night falls and then hunting through the night before finding a shady resting place at dawn.

vegetation of the Mshabene running past near-by concealed bushbuck, duiker, nyala and monkeys. All in all, it was a perfect place for the mother leopard to abandon her cubs.

The male cub, always the more independent of the two, soon moved southwards towards Hobbit's Hole (so named because of a large, gnarled old tree riddled with holes that could have concealed Hobbits!) where he had his second encounter with prey, this time a family of warthogs. We found him one clear winter day lying next to a well-used antbear hole on the side of a termite mound. There was obviously some creature inside the hole as the leopard was staring alertly at the opening, ears pricked, waiting for something to emerge.

We attempted to wait as patiently as the leopard and just when we were beginning to lose interest the action began. In an enormous cloud of dust a family of warthogs exploded out of the hole, catching us – but not the leopard – by surprise. Almost too quickly for our eyes to follow, he caught one of the warthogs by the leg at which it let out a loud, anguished squeal. The mother hog, on hearing her baby in distress, immediately charged at the leopard, her formidable tusks prominent through the dust. Leaping out of the way to avoid being gored, the leopard dropped the piglet which ran off squealing and none the worse for its terrifying experience. The young leopard looked sheepishly towards the disappearing hogs and then turned and walked slowly off in the opposite direction.

We never saw him again after this incident and we often wondered whether we would know him if we did. We certainly did not recognize the strange leopard that caused some excitement at the camp in August 1982.

At Londolozi, the day begins for the guests when one of the rangers stumbles out of bed about an hour before sunrise and gropes about in the darkness, knocking on doors and coaxing reluctant bodies on to the verandah for a cup of tea before starting on the early morning drive. On this occasion, it was Ian Thomas's turn and, having been up with his guests until late the night before, he was still struggling to keep his eyes open when he approached room number five. Suddenly he noticed an unfamiliar shape in the path in front of him. It was a leopard crouched over a freshly killed bushbuck ram. Ian and the leopard, both rooted to the spot, stared at each other and then the leopard suddenly bolted, streaking over the flower beds between room five and the camp verandah and disappearing into the reeds in the riverbed below.

Wide awake now, Ian completed his rounds, warning everyone at the camp of the presence of the leopard and then enlisting help to remove the kill to a spot in the riverbed that was visible from the verandah. That night, aided by spotlights, the guests were able to sit on the verandah and view the leopard feeding on her kill, but she was too shy to allow us any closer.

Whitebacked vulture at sunset.

It was during that August that the number of sightings of strange leopards began to increase and this made us wonder how many others there were in the area and how we could identify each individual. We knew of studies of other predators, particularly lions, in which researchers had used portrait photographs of the animals showing various scars, cuts and ear nicks that helped to identify them. Whisker spots – the marks at the point where a cat's whiskers meet the face – were also used successfully and we decided to try something similar in the identification of leopards.

There is a great truth in the old saying that a leopard never changes its spots. Besides, each leopard has its own particular spot-pattern much as every human has a unique set of fingerprints. A close look at a leopard reveals that there are black stripes where the whiskers meet the face and, just above them, a row of spots, usually two or three but varying in number, spacing, size and symmetry from leopard to leopard. We decided to use these spots as the basis of our identification system.

We began by studying photographs of the mother leopard's face. She had two spots on either side, a large nick at the top of her left ear and, across her right nostril, a very distinct scar from her clash with the male in August 1981. We then examined photographs that we had taken earlier of Sticknyawo's sister and found that although she had the same number of spots as her mother on either side of her face, their spacing and size were slightly different. Photographs of Sticknyawo, on the other hand, showed that she had three spots on the left side and two on the right. As we collected more photographs, we realized that we had devised a perfect system of identification.

From then on, all the rangers equipped themselves with cameras and flashguns and began to take portrait photographs of every leopard they saw. Over the years, this, together with the many photographs sent to us by guests, has resulted in a unique collection of identikit photographs to which we can refer whenever a leopard is sighted. It has also helped us to build up a more detailed knowledge of the leopard's ecology.

Meanwhile, the young female from the second litter had remained in the Big Dam area. She had made her first kill, a large rock monitor, at the end of August 1982. After that, she moved south-eastwards into the Tortoise Road area.

We knew that she was well on her way to adulthood in September when she made three major kills, beginning with a duiker and following it with a fully mature bushbuck female. Then, at the end of the month, she killed a young impala; she seemed to be a much more successful hunter than Sticknyawo ever was. One morning in October we arrived in the Big Dam area and found that she had killed two young impala and hoisted them into separate trees. We returned in the afternoon to discover that she had added to her larder for there was a dead monkey in a third tree nearby. However, her prowess as a killer seemed to go to her head for towards the end of the same month we found our little leopard, a 30 kilogram lightweight and an optimist if ever there was one, stalking a herd of 300 buffalo, with each individual buffalo weighing about 650 kilograms. She managed to follow the herd through the long grass without being discovered but when she was almost in their midst a few of the buffalo sensed her presence and turned to stare at her as though they could not believe the audacity of this intruder. The rest of the herd then realized that something unusual was afoot and they, too, stared at her until eventually they decided to put an end to the game. With dust flying, almost the entire herd of 300 buffalo stampeded directly towards the small leopard but, with a calmness that did not reflect the danger she was in, she casually leapt into a knob-thorn tree, clambered up to the higher branches and stared back at the herd.

The tragedy of drought.

We were to see this kind of behaviour from young leopards again and again in the ensuing years. It appears that they learn most of their hunting techniques from experience, stalking and chasing anything they can find from a mouse to an elephant. In this way they hone their skills over a period of months until eventually they find that they are actually able to catch and kill some of the smaller prey. It is only from bad experiences that they discover that there are certain animals, such as buffalo, that cannot be meddled with. Needless to say, we never witnessed our young female leopard stalk a herd of buffalo again although we did see her make an attempt on a herd of giraffe and, on another occasion, on a rhinoceros.

That September we found a pair of leopards mating in Schwein Donga, a deep gully in the south of Londolozi which is covered with dense thickets of bramble-like thorn-scrub called *Acacia schweinfurthii*. Our glimpse of the pair was sufficient to enable us to identify the female as the mother leopard and we realized that if this mating led to conception we might be lucky enough to see another litter of cubs being raised. We made a careful note of the date (12 September 1982) and, calculating on a gestation period of three-and-a-half months, we estimated that the cubs would be born around Christmas.

With growing anticipation, we began to count the days, hoping that the mother leopard would show herself towards Christmas time. However, there was one question that we kept asking ourselves. Where, we wondered, was the male leopard that was fathering these cubs? The only adult males that we had seen till then were so shy that we had merely glimpsed them briefly, with the result that it had been impossible to identify any one of them. However, one afternoon in October 1982, Warren Samuels, a newly arrived ranger from Kenya, was with Kimbian and a group of guests when they got a very good sighting of a large male leopard near Big Dam. Warren was the only ranger to see the leopard that afternoon and when he returned to camp he told us all about it.

It seemed that as he and his party crossed the Mshabene just below Big Dam he noticed what he thought was a lioness walking away from them along the riverbed. As he turned the Land Rover into the sand to follow it Kimbian, in great excitement, exclaimed that the animal was no lioness but actually a very large leopard. As the vehicle drew closer, Warren saw that Kimbian was correct: it was the largest leopard he had ever seen and he could clearly identify it as a male. After ambling along for a few yards, it turned its head towards the Land Rover and Warren was taken aback to see that it had the most grotesque face he had ever seen on a cat. It was so ugly that the leopard seemed like some creature from a horror film: above its right eyebrow there was the slash of a large black scar and, below it, the top of the right eyelid appeared to have been ripped away, leaving the yellow eyeball exposed and staring. The leopard looked at the party in the Land Rover for a second and then turned and continued walking. It had enormous powerful shoulders, a thick neck with a flap of skin hanging loosely under its throat and running along its deep chest.

It was then that Warren made a mistake. He had forgotten that this was not one of the relaxed females that had become accustomed to the Land Rovers and, hoping to give his guests a better view, he circled to approach the leopard from the front. As soon as it saw the vehicle in its path, the leopard ran straight at it, snarling and hissing and growling at the same time. That charge caught Warren totally by surprise. One second the animal was walking calmly along the riverbed; the next it was an aggressive bundle of teeth and claws hurtling at the Land Rover. Luckily Warren was able to get the Land Rover quickly into reverse and he backed out of the riverbed as fast as he could. What happened to the leopard after that he never discovered for he was too terrified to go back and find out.

Warren's sighting was recorded in our notebooks as the first positive identification of a male. We did not know what could have caused the injuries to his face but we suspected that they must have resulted from a clash with another leopard. However, no matter what was responsible, the scars would enable us to identify him quite easily in the future. We were now anxious to know whether he was the territorial male for the area and also if he could be the father of the cubs. We looked forward to further sightings of him.

That year, drought came upon us stealthily. The rainless winter months from May to September were over and the earth was thirsting for the first summer rains which usually fell in October. The herbivores had grazed the previous season's grass growth down to the ground and the grey, leafless trees stood like huge gnarled hands reaching up to the sky, begging for water. But the rains were often late and we patiently waited as, day after day, the sun rose in a clear sky and burnt itself across the parched earth before setting in the oranges and reds of the dust on the western horizon. October ended, and still there was no sign of a cloud, let alone a drop of rain. By the middle of November, the herbivores had begun to show signs of starvation: the ribs and hipbones of impala, kudu, buffalo and warthog showed gauntly under their skin. In December, huge thunderclouds built up almost daily on the western horizon but, unfulfilled promises, they soon dissipated, causing little more than an increase in humidity which made the heat that much more unbearable.

Female animals unable to withstand the twin stresses of pregnancy and drought began to die first. We started finding more and more impala carcasses, many of them females in the process of giving birth. Pregnant warthogs went into their holes to produce young and never came out. Skeleton-thin nyala began to wander into the camp in broad daylight, devouring the plants growing there and completely losing their fear of man in their desperate search for food. Many of them collapsed and died there. In the riverine vegetation along the banks of the dongas, the last places where browse was still available, we found dozens of dead bushbuck and kudu. To the south, where once there was long rank grass for the buffalo to feed on, there was nothing on the bare earth but dry stubble. Everywhere we went, the air was thick with the smell of death.

These were ideal conditions for the predators. The buffalo, so weakened by lack of food that they could offer no resistance, were easy prey, the lions moving into the herds and picking off two or three at a time, feeding on them for a while and then following the herds again.

We began to find carcasses in the mud around waterholes that were slowly drying up. In an attempt to get to the last remaining water, many animals, too weak to extricate themselves from the mud, had died. But drinking water was not the problem, as there was still plenty in the Sand River flowing past the camp. The main need was rain to infuse life into the plants that the animals depended on for their survival. The beginning of December came and went and still there was no rain.

To add to our despondency, we were getting almost no sightings of the mother leopard. We saw her once in November and again at the beginning of December. Still, we counted the days to Christmas with excitement, searching all the areas where we had regularly seen her in the months before. But Christmas came and went and still there were no signs of her.

New Year's Day 1983 dawned on us with a clear sky and a blazing sun. By 8 o'clock in the morning the haze was already rising from the bare earth. A New Year party the night before ensured that no one was up for the morning game drive and it was only at 5 o'clock in the afternoon, with the shimmering heat still hanging in the air, that we finally managed to get everyone into the Land Rovers and out of the camp. Each ranger went his separate way, some to look for lions, others in search of elephant. Three of us, Guy Arkell, Ian Thomas and I, decided on one more check of the mother leopard's old haunts. Fifteen minutes after we left the camp, the two-way radio crackled into life: Guy was calling us with the news that he had found the mother leopard walking southwards from Circuit Road Pan. With rising spirits, I turned my Land Rover around and headed in that direction. Sure enough, there she was, walking purposefully through *Combretum* woodland towards Big Dam, scent-marking against trees every few metres as she went. Her behaviour was identical to that we had noticed when following her to her previous litter. In addition, we could see quite clearly that she was lactating heavily for the pure white fur under her belly was fluffed out and swollen. We knew then that she was on her way to a lair and to a new litter of cubs.

We followed the mother leopard for about half an hour and, just as the sun set and the first scops owl began to call, she lay down near a pile of dead brush very close to Big Dam. After a few minutes she got up, stretched, and disappeared into the back of the brush-pile. We sat silently for a few minutes, listening. Then we heard the sound of soft but unmistakable high-pitched chirps, a little like a cross between a growl and a mew, emanating from the brush-pile. Carefully we manoeuvred the Land Rovers into position and just as we reached the back of the brush-pile the trackers clicked their fingers in excitement. There, clambering about in the branches on the edge, was a small leopard cub. Its eyes were open but we guessed it to be no more than two weeks old. As it scrambled out of sight, we could hear at least one other cub chirping from inside the brush. We were ecstatic – we couldn't have asked for a better start to the New Year. We waited for a few more minutes, but saw and heard nothing further as the gathering darkness slowly engulfed us.

We visited the brush-pile daily, hoping for more sightings of the cubs, but saw nothing until 4 January when we arrived just in time to see the mother moving from the lair with something dangling from her mouth. When we were closer, we realized that she was carrying one of the cubs, holding it not by the scruff of the neck but with the head inside her mouth. This was another 'first' for us. We had never before seen a leopard carrying a cub; it was something we suspected was done only in the greatest secrecy in the dead of night. We suspected too that the cubs would be carried only during the first weeks of their lives before they were fully mobile. This meant that there was only a very short period in the life of a leopard when one would have a chance of seeing it being carried. On this occasion the mother carried the cub for approximately another 200 metres and then disappeared into another brush-pile in a gully closer to Big Dam. We waited there, hoping that she would return and fetch the other cub, but there was no sound or movement. As we left the area Carlson, my tracker, sat on the bonnet of the Land Rover carefully scanning the route that the leopard had followed. From the tracks, he was able to deduce that she had walked back and forth two or three times and so we assumed that she had already moved the first cub by the time we had arrived.

Our first real sighting of this new litter of cubs, as described at the beginning of this book, came at the beginning of February after a remarkable piece of tracking by Carlson. We were on the lip of a donga overlooking a pile of granite boulders where the

A male lion kicks up a cloud of dust as he sets out on his evening hunt through a recently burnt area. Sleeping off and on from sunrise until sunset, lions are almost exclusively active at night and pose a major threat to leopards.

ABOVE AND RIGHT: *Under pressure from a hyaena, a female leopard struggles to hoist an almost intact female impala, weighing as much as she does, into a tree.*

cubs tumbled and played, and, next to us, in a low *Acacia* tree, was a small cup-shaped bird's nest with two naked chicks in it. After a few minutes the rattle of wings signified the arrival of the parent bird, a threestreaked tchagra, which immediately deposited some food into the chicks' gaping beaks and then flew off again. To the south of us, baboons were barking among themselves while, circling high in the pale blue sky, dozens of vultures signified the death of yet another animal. The hot air hung breathlessly about us as we watched the cubs and listened to the sounds within the surrounding bush. This, despite the drought, was Londolozi at its best. For the alert and observant, there was always something happening.

February that year produced the best viewing of the leopard cubs we had ever had – there were only three days in the month that we did not see them. The mother kept them in the lair among the granite boulders for nine days before moving them and it was during this time that we got to know her contact call – a single low grunt repeated now and again as she returned to the lair site after a hunt. On hearing it, the cubs would suddenly stop their play or emerge from their hiding places. They would listen for a second call and then, answering with high-pitched chirps, would go bounding off in the direction of the sound. Often the only clue we had of the mother's arrival was the sudden pricking of the cubs' ears in response to a call which had eluded our hearing. On meeting the mother, the cubs would greet her by rubbing their bodies against her and she would respond by licking them firmly before lying down and allowing them to suckle.

The cubs were at their most vulnerable when the mother was away hunting. They were still too small to climb trees rapidly so their only means of defence was to disappear into small cracks among the boulders where they could safely hide from predators. There were numbers of hyaena in the area, but even more dangerous was the ever-present threat of two prides of lions that regularly moved in the vicinity of the lair. Whenever we found lions nearby, we watched their movements with concern, hoping that they would not go near the lair and wondering what we would do if they did. But the mother leopard had chosen the site well and the lions never did find the cubs there. Surprisingly, it was the mother leopard, out hunting on her own, who first came under attack from a lioness.

Pete le Roux, a young biologist who had recently joined us and who hoped to complete his studies with a thesis on the subject of leopards, was following her late one afternoon as she hunted near the southern boundary of Londolozi. She had stopped to rest in the shade of a jacket-plum tree and was looking across an open space towards a herd of impala in the distance when Pete's tracker spotted a lioness behind their Land Rover. The lioness must have been watching the mother leopard for some time for, when they saw it, it was in the process of stalking

Adult male common duiker.

her, hardly 50 metres away, its body tense, feet advancing slowly, ears pricked forward and eyes fixed on its prey. As the lioness moved closer, the leopard, losing interest in the impala, lay down next to the tree, completely oblivious of the impending threat.

Pete was facing the dilemma that we had experienced when Sticknyawo was struggling. Should he move forward, make a noise and so warn the leopard of the approaching danger, or should he sit back and watch nature take its course? Possibly because he had not known the leopard for as long as we had and therefore felt less emotional about her, but more probably because he was a scientist who tended to look at things in an objective way, Pete decided on the latter alternative.

When the lioness was about 10 metres away, she charged at the leopard, catching her totally unawares. With a loud growling, the two cats disappeared in a cloud of dust behind some bushes and, at first, Pete was unable to make out what had happened. The dust disturbed by the clashing cats hung in the air for a few seconds and then cleared to reveal the panting lioness gazing towards a grove of trees. Pete had no idea how the leopard had managed to escape, for he had been sure that she was doomed, but he saw her perched high up in the branches of a sturdy tamboti tree, panting heavily and staring at the lioness below.

Ten minutes passed, then the lioness left the area and Pete continued to follow the leopard as she headed down towards the Mshabene. In the darkness, half an hour after her narrow escape, she killed an adult male impala, dragged it into a thicket and then lay down to rest before feeding on it.

Two days later, the mother leopard moved her cubs once again. We arrived at the lair only to find her making her way down the donga with two of the cubs while the third lagged some distance behind. As we watched, she leapt up on to the opposite bank of the donga; two of the cubs were able to scramble up after her but the smallest cub kept tumbling back into the gully. The mother returned to the edge of the bank and, giving the contact call, looked down at the cub. When she realized that it was struggling to climb the bank, she reached down with one front paw and gently hooked the cub up towards her. Once it was safely beside her, the mother picked it up and carried it to a small termite mound not more than 50 metres from the rocks where the other two cubs were already ensconced.

The mother leopard kept the cubs in the new lair for four days and then took them to a brush-pile in the Mshabene. Early the following morning we found her on the move again, this time taking the cubs upstream to a pile of large granite boulders some 500 metres from the previous lair site, where she settled down to suckle them.

It was while the mother leopard and the cubs were on these rocks that we saw one of the many interesting interactions that often occur between the leopards and other animals in the area. For some time, a dark chanting goshawk had been perched on a dead tree scanning the ground for potential prey. Then a crested francolin came strutting out of the bush nearby and began to move further and further into the open, while the goshawk waited patiently for the right moment to swoop. Eventually, when the francolin was at the furthest point from any protective patch of bush, the goshawk launched itself downwards from its perch, its wings whistling in the wind as it picked up speed.

It seemed to have its timing right, but the francolin reacted with a shrill alarm call and a short level flight low over the ground into the long dense grass among the branches of a fallen tree. The goshawk was close on the francolin's heels but just too late to get its talons into its

Lesser bushbaby.

prey. Nevertheless, it did not give up and began walking round the tree in an attempt to get at the francolin. By this time, the leopard had noticed the commotion. She sprang up from her position on the rock and raced towards the fallen tree, sending the goshawk flying. Then she spent at least 15 minutes trying to get at the francolin, while all the while the bird gave its shrill alarm call from the depths of the long grass beneath the tree. Finally, the francolin managed to emerge from behind the fallen tree and fly safely away.

The three cubs were first taken to a kill when they were just over two months old. The victim was an adult female impala and the mother had hoisted the carcass high into the branches of a large jackal-berry tree under which we found her resting while the cubs suckled. After some time the mother rose and, with graceful ease, leapt into the tree to feed on the kill. It was then that we realized the kill was not only safe from scavengers, it was also out of reach of the little cubs, for they tried again and again, but always in vain, to climb up the thick straight tree trunk.

They called in frustration for a while, but then gave up and turned to their games. The two larger cubs robustly chased and tumbled after each other while the smaller one, showing more finesse, stalked slowly after them, lay in wait, pounced and stalked again. As the mother fed, the tail of the impala suddenly dropped off the carcass and fell among the cubs. The largest cub grabbed it and carried it like a trophy to a small tree which he proceeded to climb up and down, the tail dangling from his mouth. As he played his little game, the second cub tried to grab the tail from him and an aggressive fight ensued, with much loud growling, snarling and hissing. The mother instantly leapt out of the tree and, snarling silently and aggressively, thrust her head between her fighting offspring. After a minute or so, they quietened down and the mother returned to her feeding.

The importance of this behaviour was obvious to us. Had the fight continued, the growling would have attracted any scavengers that might have been within earshot. The threat posed by

a lion or hyaena in the vicinity of her small cubs was something the mother leopard simply could not risk. Hence her determination to end the cubs' noisy fight.

Two days later, we visited the site of the kill to find that the leopards had already left, but Carlson and Kimbian expertly picked up their footprints and we began following. The tracks headed westwards through the woodland, eventually leading into the Mshabene some distance downstream from Big Dam. After following the trail along the riverbed for a short distance, Carlson indicated a large paw-print in the sand. It was the track of a full-grown male leopard, and it appeared that he had joined up with the mother and her cubs.

This was a new development as we had always understood that male leopards had nothing to do with the females or their offspring once mating had taken place. We studied the tracks carefully as we wanted to make sure that the male had indeed joined the female. After a while Carlson and Kimbian determined that there were tracks of the male leopard both underneath and on top of the cub tracks, meaning that the male must have been moving together with them and their mother. For two days after that we found their tracks with those of the male: something more of the leopard mystery had been revealed to us.

At the beginning of April, when the cubs were just over four months old, the mother leopard took them to the carcass of an adult female impala that she had dragged to the foot of a marula tree. She allowed the cubs to feed first while she rested nearby. The following evening, when we arrived to watch them, we found them in an extremely playful mood. They chased around after one another, climbed up small saplings that collapsed under their weight, pounced on the kill, on top of the mother and on top of one another. They stalked the Land Rovers, played with the mother's tail, and 'killed' the impala carcass again and again. They clumsily used clumps of grass and bush to hide in as they playfully stalked and chased and fought, the mother all the while resting aloofly in the branches of the marula. There was not one person among the 30 or more viewing them that evening who was not completely captivated by the antics of the three little cubs.

That night, the lions that had been on the prowl for so long finally made good their threats. Warren and Kimbian made the tragic discovery early the next morning. Approaching the area of the impala kill, they picked up tracks of three lionesses heading straight towards the place where they had left the cubs the night before. About 100 metres away, they found the first dead cub and 100 metres further on, a second with the mother leopard lying, resting, next to it. Both cubs had bite marks on their heads and bodies and there were lion tracks all over the ground. Filled with apprehension, Warren and Kimbian looked around them but at first there was no sign of the third cub.

Obviously, the lions had smelt the kill and had come to investigate, hoping to scavenge a little meat. But the impala carcass was still dangling safely in the higher branches of the marula tree where it had been hoisted earlier, well out of reach of the lions. However, because of their youth and inexperience, the cubs had obviously been too slow to respond to the mortal danger posed by the lions' approach.

We were all devastated. It came to us as a great shock to find the little characters dead for only the previous evening the cubs had provided us with such happy entertainment and we were, of course, looking forward to enjoying so much more. The guests especially were overwhelmed by the brutality of it all.

We drove through the bush in circles, frantically looking for any sign of the third cub and all the while hoping against hope that she was still alive. At last we found her some 200 metres away from the kill site. Obviously terrified and quite unable to move, she was wedged into the highest branches of a red bushwillow tree. We watched her for a few minutes and then, afraid that the presence of the Land Rovers might frighten her from her place of safety, we returned to the place where we had left the mother resting beside one of the dead cubs. The bizarre scene that followed shocked us all and posed a number of new unanswered questions.

As we watched, the mother leopard picked up the dead cub, carried it northwards across the Mshabene and hoisted it into a large jackal-berry tree on the riverbank. After wedging it into the branches, she returned to the second dead cub and carried it towards the Mshabene for a short distance before depositing it on the ground. She sat up for a moment, looked around, and then, kneeling down, began to feed on it.

We were stunned. Less than 12 hours earlier, the mother leopard had been grooming and suckling and playing affectionately with her little cubs. And now she was eating one of them. We had heard of cannibalism in lions, but this was the first recorded instance, as far as we knew, of cannibalism in leopards. Somehow we had imagined the princely leopard to be above this sort of behaviour. But the mother ate the cub just as if it were an impala, a duiker or any other source of meat, the only difference being that she seemed to be feeding much more carefully. Every now and then she stopped to bare her teeth in a silent snarl known as a flehmen face, giving the appearance that the meat was distasteful, and then she would settle down to feed again. After consuming more than half of the carcass, she carried the remains into another jackal-berry tree some 50 metres from where she had deposited the first cub. She rested in the tree and groomed herself for a few minutes before returning to the kill.

She called regularly, alternating between her territorial call and the cub contact call in an obvious attempt to locate the third cub. But the little animal must have been too afraid to respond, for it kept completely silent. The mother, still calling, leapt into the marula tree and fed on the impala carcass before stretching herself out on one of the branches and went to sleep. The cub, in the meantime, had dared to climb down from the tree and was now hiding in a dense thicket on top of a termite mound.

Eventually she gave one or two very soft contact calls which the mother apparently could not hear, and then kept silent.

For the rest of the day, the mother leopard spent her time alternating between the three carcasses, feeding on the impala, then moving down to the Mshabene to feed on the two cubs, before returning to the impala, calling forlornly all the while.

It was only on the second day after the tragedy that we found the mother and her cub reunited. They were together in the Mshabene near one of the carcasses and the remaining cub was suckling from the mother. For the next three days they remained in this area, the strange thing being that the mother kept on calling, almost as though she was still seeking her missing cubs.

Five days after the death of the cubs, we followed her as she moved with the cub up to the head of Three-streaked Donga, for the first time leaving the vicinity of her dead offspring. She left the remaining cub on a termite mound; then she moved southwards again, back towards the place where she had hoisted the two little carcasses, calling continually as she went. When she reached the Mshabene, she sat on top of a termite mound and, looking towards the trees where the dead cubs had been hoisted, called again. After a few minutes of this behaviour, she moved still further southwards to the place where the cubs had been killed, calling all the while. With considerable sadness, we realized that she was still looking for her missing cubs which by now had been completely consumed. She continued behaving in this way for two more days, searching and calling, searching and calling until finally, a full week after the tragedy, the calling subsided and the mother leopard moved out of the area.

During this time, there was an atmosphere of gloom at Londolozi. It was almost as though there had been a death among us and everyone was trying to come to terms with his personal grief. The situation was a very difficult one to understand and was made even more complicated by the ease with which we ascribed human emotions to animal behaviour. There were even those who described the leopard as being 'sad' or 'in mourning'. However, most of us felt strongly that such feelings could not be ascribed to the leopard or, for that matter, to any wild animal.

But why, we kept asking ourselves, had the mother leopard eaten her cubs? Perhaps she had been driven to it by the stress that she was under, perhaps she was trying to hide evidence of the carcasses in case scavengers picked up the smell, or perhaps she saw the carcasses simply as another source of meat. Was she aware that she was eating her own cubs? It was obvious from the way that she had searched for them after eating them that she had made no connection between them and the meat that she had consumed.

But this raised another question. How does the mother recognize her cubs? Is it through smell, sight, sound or touch, or is it a combination of all these senses with a variety of cues providing the recognition signals? If recognition depended on smell alone, then the mother would surely have known her own cubs even though they were dead. However it was always possible that all the senses came into play and that the mother needed a variety of cues such as calls, physical contact, milk utilization, smells and body language in order to recognize her cubs. Whatever the explanation, it was apparent that she was unaware that the dead cubs were her own. It seemed that her maternal instincts had persisted for about a week after the death of the cubs and had only then subsided. Perhaps this seemingly intuitive behaviour had been hormonally controlled and, now that the cues that had stimulated it were no longer acting, the mother's maternal instincts gradually declined until she event-ually 'forgot' about her missing cubs and finally moved away from the area to care for the one that remained.

This episode had opened up a whole new area of the leopard's life to us, an aspect that had never before been described. While it was upsetting to have lost the two cubs, it would also be very interesting to know what had driven the mother leopard to act as she did. While we still had no definite answers, we felt, day by day and month by month, that we were steadily developing a deeper understanding of leopard behaviour.

ABOVE: *Alertly protective of her cubs, a female leopard stares up at a pair of African hawk eagles passing overhead. Although there are no records of large birds of prey taking leopard cubs, they pose a potential threat.*
OVERLEAF: *An elegant young female leopard stretches out along a branch.*

A leopard pauses during a drink as the early morning sun shimmers through water dripping from her mouth.

*The quintessential leopard. Shadowy figures at a waterhole, their eyes glowing in the light
of the flash, these two leopards appeared out of the darkness, drank and then disappeared once more
into the night. Photographs such as this, rather than the more commonly seen brightly lit portraits,
are subtly evocative of the shy, elusive nature of these secretive cats.*

LEFT: *This is a rare sight for cubs are carried to new lairs by the mother only during the first month of their lives and invariably at night. From the second month, the young leopards are strong enough to follow the mother.*
ABOVE: *Three-month-old leopard cub.*

LEFT: *During an early morning hunt, the mother leopard pauses to survey the landscape from a fallen tree.*
ABOVE: *In graceful full flight, an impala escapes potential danger. Because the impala is the most abundant prey species at Londolozi, predators often encounter these animals and considerable numbers are killed. Being of a size and weight that the leopard can deal with, they make up more than 50 per cent of its diet.*

After a heavy feed, a pride of lions settles down to drink, one of them with a fresh wound possibly from a clash with a horned animal like a wildebeest or buffalo. Lions are the only truly social cats, moving in closely-knit family groups led by females, with adult males playing an important territorial role.

We had never heard of cannibalism in leopards before this occasion when the mother leopard lost two out of three cubs to lions in a single night. Here she carries one half-eaten cub through the bush to the Mshabene where she stashed it into a jackal-berry tree before returning to feed on the second cub.

AGGRESSION

The drought, which had now spread over most of southern Africa, relentlessly tightened its grip on the land. Experts were describing it as 'the worst in living memory' and at Londolozi, where the average annual rainfall is 600 millimetres, a mere 250 fell in a period of 18 months. The result was a starvation die-off of countless animals including over 5 000 impala, 300 warthog, an estimated 100 nyala, 400 bushbuck and 500 kudu. The buffalo population, which had numbered about 1 200 before the drought, dropped to 600. Many of them broke through the fence of the reserve in a frantic search for better pastures, a hundred more fell prey to the lions and the rest died of starvation.

The land was stark, grey and gloomy, and the sun beat down on the leafless landscape where long green grass had once stood. There were so many carcasses everywhere that the satiated scavengers could not dispose of them all, leaving them to the sun and the maggots. The last real chance of rain disappeared with the month of April 1983, after which we had to wait five months or so before we could expect the drought to be broken. Most of the weaker animals had died by then and the few remaining probably had enough food and resilience to see them through the difficult months ahead.

The drought did not seem to affect the leopards at all. If anything, it probably made life a little easier for them, the weaker prey animals being easier to catch and the lions and hyaenas being less of a threat because of the ready availability of carcasses.

Most of our attention at this stage was centred on the mother with her remaining cub, but every now and then we would get another sighting of the young female from her previous litter. At first, we found her near the centre of the mother's territory but, as the hot, dry months passed, she gradually moved south-eastwards into the area into which Sticknyawo had moved a year before. The main watercourse running through it and providing ideal habitat for leopards is the Tugwaan, a large deep donga that follows the southern boundary of Londolozi. At the bottom, there are dense thickets of *Acacia schweinfurthii*, piles of granite boulders in places and, lining the banks, beautiful examples of large jackal-berry trees, sausage trees, mahoganies and tambotis. All in all, a perfect place for a leopard to set up territory.

The young female announced the onset of her sexual maturity by starting to give the repeated grunting territorial call at the beginning of September 1983 when she was just over two years old. After that, we did not see her for three weeks, so we had no idea whether any interaction followed with other leopards in the area.

When we next sighted her at the end of September we found her in extremely poor condition: her hipbones and ribs were protruding, her coat was dull and lifeless and there was a vacancy in her eyes. Ironically, she was lying next to Sticknyawo's Pan and we hoped that history was not about to repeat itself.

As she lay there, a squirrel, unaware of her presence, came hopping across a branch in a knob-thorn tree above her. The young leopard watched it intently as it moved slowly down the tree towards her. When it was some two metres above her, she leapt up into the tree in a desperate attempt to catch it. But she was much too slow, and the squirrel scampered up into the higher branches, well out of her reach. Nevertheless, the leopard had not given up. Clambering clumsily upwards she tried to cut off the squirrel's escape but, just as she seemed to be getting the upper hand, she lost her balance and came crashing down through the branches, hitting the ground with a thud. This gave us some indication of how weak she really was for an accident of this kind would never have happened to a leopard in peak condition. When we left her, she was walking slowly eastwards, scent-marking every so often against trees and bushes.

Her expression the epitome of aggression, the Sand River female prepares to leap from a marula tree.
The few hostile encounters we experienced usually involved a female leopard that was protecting small cubs. However,
certain individuals, such as this female, do display an unpredictable temperament.

We could only guess at the reason for her poor condition. Perhaps it was a 'catch-22' situation – an illness that had weakened her and thus affected her hunting abilities. This, combined with lack of food, had weakened her yet further and we wondered how she was going to break out of this vicious circle.

At last, in October it rained. It started slowly at first, a gentle soaking drizzle that lasted for two days and brought the sweet and wonderful smell of moisture that we had all but forgotten. Within three days of that first rain, green shoots of grass had sprung up all over the bush in places where, for the last 18 months, there had been nothing but sand. Bright green buds appeared on the trees and tortoises came scuttling from their hiding places as fast as they could to satisfy their thirst at any little puddle they could find. The feeling of elation that we

The beautiful lion's eye flower.

all experienced after so many rainless months is very difficult to describe. Suffice to say that we all, staff and guests at Londolozi, simply stood in the rain and allowed the wonderful wetness to soak our bodies.

A week later, after four days of stiflingly hot weather, a build-up of purple storm clouds in the west promised more rain. Within hours of their appearance, they darkened the landscape and finally released their load. In the space of two days 100 millimetres of rain had fallen and the drought was really over at last. As those early summer days went by, the colour of the landscape quickly changed from browns and greys to various shades of brilliant green. A verdant lawn developed under the trees and the once leafless branches drooped under the weight of lush green foliage.

For me, the months of October and November, when the first rains have fallen, are the best in the year. There are colourful little wild flowers on the ground, yellow blossoms in the trees and new green leaves and grass everywhere. Birds become more vociferous as their courtship begins and impala, warthog and wildebeest start to drop their young. It is a time of new beginnings and this year, with the breaking of the drought, these new beginnings were especially significant.

And the rain was not the only good news. In the middle of October 1983, we found the young female leopard on an adult impala kill. She was in perfect health and spent a full four days feeding on the carcass which she had hoisted into a marula tree safely out of reach of scavengers. It was at this time that we got our first real inkling of the unpredictable behaviour of leopards. For three days all the game drives viewed her and she revealed the calm tolerance of the Land Rovers that she and her mother had always shown. On the fourth day, Pete le Roux visited her on his own in order to take some portrait photographs to add to the identikit collection. He had stopped the Land Rover next to her kill and had just raised his camera to his face when she suddenly snarled aggressively at him. As Pete started up the vehicle, she charged, rushing at him with a low darting run, front legs splayed outwards as she came. Fortunately, Pete already had the vehicle in reverse and the leopard, seeing it retreating, called off her charge. Later we were to learn that this aggressive behaviour seemed to be a trait of the young female.

The episode taught us two things. First, we could never take the leopards' acceptance of the Land Rovers for granted. We were to find that there would always be times when they would show less tolerance, charging if we came too close. These occasions were largely unpredictable but we began to think that they were related to cyclical changes occurring in the leopard's body, such as oestrus, or to the presence of young cubs. We learnt that it was very important always to approach any leopard slowly and carefully, watching her reaction to the vehicle and backing off at any sign of aggression: flattened ears, a fixed stare or a flicking tail.

Secondly, the incident taught us how to react if a leopard ever charged. On one occasion Kimbian was viewing the mother leopard and her small cubs with his Land Rover backed up against a large tree trunk when the mother suddenly stood up and charged. Unable to back out, Kimbian could only sit inside the vehicle and watch, his rifle at the ready. The leopard lunged forward five or six times and for a few minutes it was touch and go as to whether or not she would leap into the Land Rover. Fortunately for everyone, she eventually turned her back and disappeared into the bush, but from that moment onwards we knew that our best course of action was to back out the moment a leopard threatened.

Together with the trackers, we spent a great deal of time on foot following leopard tracks and there was always the risk that one of them might charge. Here again, from personal experience we discovered that our best course of action when charged by a leopard is to back off. We had previously had far more experience of tracking lions and in our aggressive encounters with them had always held our ground, staring back at the lion as it charged. The lion invariably stopped a few metres away and then stared back at us for what seemed like long minutes before turning tail. This was a nerve-racking experience that always left us with knees trembling, but it worked.

I soon found that this treatment could not be applied to leopards. Early one morning, Carlson and I left the Land Rover to search for the mother leopard and her cub in a fairly dense patch of scented thorn where they had been seen the night before. We wandered about separately in the thicket looking for tracks until eventually Carlson's low whistle indicated to me that he had found something. When I joined him, he pointed out the mother's track heading towards the bank of the Mshabene.

I loaded my rifle and followed him as he carefully worked the tracks. When we reached the bank, which was almost vertical at this point, Carlson began to climb down towards the riverbed below. He was halfway over the edge when I saw the leopard lying in a patch of long grass not more than two metres from me. Her head was low and her ears were flat as she stared back at me. I whispered urgently to Carlson and he immediately came back to the top of the bank.

The moment Carlson joined me, she came at us with a deep grunting growl, her body low to the ground and her front legs spread apart as though in readiness to grab us. Less than a metre away, she veered sideways in a cloud of dust and we thought that the charge was over, but she just retreated a metre or so and then came at us again. She repeated this action three more times before we decided to back off, scrambling backwards down the vertical bank of the Mshabene, not once removing our eyes from the leopard and ripping our shirts against the thorn trees as we went. It was a truly frightening experience and we learnt from it never to stand our ground with a leopard again.

We had already seen that the leopard's relationship to lions was one of complete subordination, but how did they relate to the other big predator in the area, the cheetah? We found out one day in December 1983 when we came across a female cheetah on a freshly killed adult impala in the middle of an open clearing. We had just settled down to watch it, when the cheetah suddenly sat up and looked alertly away to the west. At first we could not see what she had seen and she quickly took a few more bites from her kill before looking up again. Then we noticed a movement in the grass. It was the mother leopard and she was stalking slowly towards the cheetah. When she was only some 20 metres away, the cheetah quickly snatched one more bite, stood up, and with a soft growl, turned tail and ran eastwards across the clearing, stopping every now and then to look back at the leopard as she went. The leopard moved in warily and when she reached the kill she grabbed it by the neck, straddled it, and dragged it into a gully at the bottom of the clearing.

This incident told us everything about the cheetah's relationship to the other predators in the area. Cheetahs are not at all robustly built: they have narrow feet, long thin bodies and small light skulls with light jaw-bones and small teeth. Hence they are no match for the more powerfully built lions, leopards and hyaenas. All these animals steal kills from a cheetah which prefers escape rather than a confrontation that could result in injury or death. Cheetahs are in fact very timid animals and there have even been reports of their being frightened off kills by large numbers of vultures.

During the next few months we watched as the mother leopard successfully raised her surviving cub. The core area of her territory was still centred around Big Dam and the Mshabene and she was having no trouble providing herself and the cub with kills. When the young leopard was nine months old, she

Raindrop on lichen-covered twig.

made her first kill, a scrub hare, and then a month later, she caught a large-spotted genet. The leopards experienced two scares during this time, both involving lions. Once we came into the area of one of their kills to find lion tracks everywhere and the mother leopard in a tree but no sign of the cub. We spent a large part of the morning looking for her but without success. We finally found her late that afternoon together with the mother near the kill.

A more serious threat followed one night in December when the mother led the cub to a baby impala that she had killed earlier. The cub had just settled down to feed when suddenly, taking her completely by surprise, a large male lion appeared. It was in its final leap when the cub realized what was happening and somehow managed to scramble from under its feet and spring to safety in a marula tree.

We often wondered whether the menace of dangerous predators in her territory would force the mother to move, but despite threats from resident lions she stayed in the same area. However, a month after the second lion incident, she moved northwards without the cub and we spent an interesting few days with her on the northern boundary of her territory.

In the Sand River, some two kilometres downstream from the camp, there is a large sheet of granite often used by the lions for resting on. In the early days, this beautiful spot was a place of relaxation and contemplation for John and Dave's father, Boyd Varty, and today there is a plaque attached to the rock in his memory. Because of this, the place was known to us as Plaque Rock and inland from the river there is an open area dotted with knob-thorn trees called Plaque Clearing. In the middle of January 1984, this area became the centre of intense mating activity involving the mother leopard and an unidentified male.

Early one morning, Warren reported the sound of leopards mating in dense bush between the river and Plaque Clearing. John Varty had just started filming the leopards and this was a unique opportunity for him to get footage of them during mating. He was in the area as soon as the report came in and spent the rest of the day following the unmistakable mating sounds through some of the densest bush he had ever known.

'It was one of the most frustrating times of my life,' he told us. 'The bush was so dense that although we were parked less than two metres from the sound of the mating we still could not see anything at all. It was almost unbearable having the camera at the ready with everything going on underneath our noses but being quite unable to film.'

It was a classic case of so near and yet so far. After each mating the leopards would part and then move on to another patch of bush, with the female leading the way. They would rest for a few minutes and then mate once again, always choosing the densest patch of bush they could find. John managed to get a successful sound recording of the leopards during the course of the night,

but no film footage at all. Finally, at two o'clock the next morning he fell into bed frustrated and exhausted.

A few hours later, before the sun had coloured the morning sky, John was out once more on the trail of the leopards. He and Elmon followed their tracks around the camp and into the riverbed at the hippo pools just upstream. There he heard them mating again, but once more the area they were in was impenetrable. With incredible determination, John remained with the leopards until late that night when they emerged from the river and began moving towards the back of the camp. Knowing that the bush in this area was less thick, John eagerly followed them but somehow the leopards found yet another dense thicket to mate in. Then they came out into the open to rest.

This, at last, was John's chance, and he carefully positioned the Land Rover and set up his equipment. After a few minutes the female got up and brushed past the male, rubbing her body against his face. But, as John switched on his filming light, disaster struck. One of the batteries powering the light suddenly burst into flames, plunging the Land Rover into darkness. As the leopards mated right in front of him, John, swearing profusely, beat the fire out with his hat. He quickly returned to camp and 15 minutes later was back with the leopards armed with a replacement battery. Doggedly, he spent the rest of the night with them and finally, at approximately two o'clock the following morning, he captured the pair of mating leopards on film. His perseverance had eventually paid off. The scene was one of the highlights of the film and, as he explained afterwards: 'It was very rewarding finally catching something on film that I knew was unique and that I had spent days trying to get in extremely difficult circumstances.'

Until this incident we believed that female leopards mated only once they had parted from their young, but in this case the cub, now 13 months old, was still very much part of the mother's life as she still supplied it with all its food. The mating continued for fully three days during which there was no inclination on the part of either leopard to hunt. On the fourth day, however, the mother was found together with the cub on two impala lambs that she had killed. There was no sign of the male, but a day later she was back with him in the river at Plaque Rock. This time the mating lasted for another two days after which the leopards went their separate ways.

In February, the mother began to show less tolerance of the cub. She would snarl at the cub every time she came close and eventually she abandoned her for the last time in the area of the Dudley-Sparta Vlei.

In March 1984, we got our first indication that the young female from the previous litter had met up with a male. She was by this time well established around the Tugwaan to the south of Londolozi and we found her on the main road to Skukuza

Imparting the qualities of a painting to this bushveld scene, late afternoon sunshine lights up the landscape as the storm clouds clear.

A young leopard is caught in mid-leap as she responds to a rustling in the grass. Leopards learn to hunt largely through play-activity: they stalk and chase anything that moves, be it a leaf blowing in the wind, an insect or even their own tails. First kills, at eight or nine months, are usually such small creatures as hares, mongoose or francolins.

An adult female leopard kills a sub-adult male impala. Most animals are killed by asphyxiation, the leopard quickly clamping her jaws round the wind-pipe and holding on until the victim stops breathing. Sometimes the leopard's teeth may pierce the jugular vein and occasionally, especially with smaller prey, the neck is broken.

showing intense territorial behaviour – scent-marking and scraping her hind feet on the ground at regular intervals. She climbed a large umbrella thorn tree, squirted a great deal of urine against the trunk, rubbed her face continually against the branches and pulled a flehmen face several times. She scraped her feet vigorously in two different places on the ground and returned to the main road where she continued to scent-mark and to rub her face against bushes at regular intervals along the way, pulling a flehmen face each time. It was then that we noticed the tracks of a large male leopard on the road and we suspected that it was his scent she was following. Perhaps, we thought, the young female was in oestrus.

By now she had started showing a little wear and tear as she had acquired two small parallel tears in her left ear and a large nick in her right. We added any details such as these to the existing information in our identikit in order to make the system more accurate.

The success of our system was brought home to us at about this time when one night, some 10 kilometres south of the mother's territory, the rangers found a strange female leopard that was very relaxed in the presence of the Land Rovers. It was very dark; in the knob-thorn trees around us pearlspotted owls regularly gave their long drawn out whistles and in the distance we occasionally heard the quiet 'trrrrroooou' of the whitefaced owl. The leopard was hunting, zigzagging through the bush, stopping every now and then to listen, and then moving on again. Four Land Rovers followed her as she continued with her hunt but she showed no interest in the vehicles whatsoever. Puzzled at this unusual tolerance from a strange leopard, we followed her, hoping to get some portrait photographs to compare with the identikit.

As we trailed her we heard the sound of animals rushing out of a hole on the far side of a termite mound. The leopard also heard the noise and turned back to investigate. We followed her and as we reached the side of the mound we saw two young warthogs. Just then, the leopard burst out of some long grass nearby and, right before our eyes, caught one of the hogs. Almost in the same instant, she leapt up into a marula tree just as the mother warthog burst out of the darkness and charged towards her. Perched in the fork of the tree, the leopard held on to the hog, one paw over its face, as she administered a fatal bite to its throat. Once the animal was dead, she hoisted it into the higher branches of the tree and, ever the opportunist, went back down to the hole to see if there were any other hogs sheltering there. Satisfied that there was nothing more to be had, she lay down in the long grass and groomed herself. As she lay there, we were able to get portrait photographs of both sides of her face.

When the pictures were returned from the processors, we compared them with those in the identikit and were delighted to find that the leopard that had given us so much excitement

Fresh leopard tracks in the sand.

that night was in fact Sticknyawo's sister. It was fully four years since we had last seen her and she had been all but forgotten. It was most exciting to know that our identification system was enabling us to renew old acquaintances.

Sticknyawo's sister had established herself in inhospitable terrain covered in dense stands of knob-thorn made even more difficult by a scattering of large dolomitic rocks. Although this area was all but impassable to Land Rovers, it was here, during the next three months, that we had a number of sightings of her. We followed her as she chased a strange leopard off a kill; we observed her while she hunted; we watched her lose a kill to a hyaena and we saw her, obviously well-established in her territory, scent-marking and scraping.

One day in June, as we watched Sticknyawo's sister resting in a marula tree, we noticed that she was lactating heavily and that her teats appeared to have been recently utilized. This was an exciting discovery: it meant that, lying up somewhere in the area, there was a litter of cubs that we knew to be the second generation of leopards descended from the mother leopard. Unfortunately, because of the nature of the terrain and because of the distance from camp, we were unable to spend much time in the area, so we never had an opportunity to follow Sticknyawo's sister to her cubs.

The hot summer months brought with them plenty of rain. It had not seemed possible that the dead, drought-stricken environment would ever recover, but it did. By the end of February 1984, the once-bare earth was completely covered in dense stands of a variety of grass species and the trees had all come back to life, many of them with their leaf-covered branches heavy with fruit. All the non-perennial pans scattered about the bush were overflowing with water, providing ideal conditions for frogs, terrapins and other waterborne life, and the herbivores, making good use of the abundance of food and water, began to look fat and healthy.

The mother leopard, during this time, had given birth to another litter of cubs, her fourth, born sometime in April 1984, which she initially kept well hidden in dense reeds in the Sand River at Plaque Rock. This river was the mother leopard's northern boundary and it appeared that she had shifted her territory northwards as she was now spending much more time in this area to the north of the main road.

At the end of May, when the new litter of cubs was only a month or so old, we found a pair of leopards mating in the river at Plaque Rock. Once again, it was extremely difficult to get any sort of sighting but eventually they came out of the river in the darkness and once more we were able to identify the female as the mother. We had until then believed that leopards came into oestrus only when their cubs had become independent or if they had all died, so we assumed that she had lost this latest litter and that she was now cycling again. The mating continued for four days and as we saw no sign of the cubs for the next few weeks we believed our assumption was correct. However, in June we found the mother leopard south of Plaque Clearing with a pair of healthy two-month-old offspring, meaning that she had mated even though she was still nursing young cubs.

Once again, this most unusual discovery generated much debate and thought among the rangers. Obviously there was something more than we fully comprehended to the leopard's oestrus cycles and we made enquiries of various experts in an attempt to get a better knowledge of what was happening. We discovered that these cycles were not completely understood, but it appeared from studies carried out in captivity that leopards come into oestrus as often as every 52 days if the initial mating does not lead to conception. This regular oestrus cycle ensures that, should her cubs die, there will not be a long hiatus before she cycles and can produce another litter. However, none of the experts had heard of leopards mating when their cubs were so young and we wondered what significance this mysterious behaviour could have.

We also wondered how we could tell when the leopard was in oestrus. Did her normal behaviour change or not? In other large cats, such as jaguar and puma, oestrus is indicated by the unusual behaviour of the cat – rolling on the ground, pacing and restlessness as well as an increase in calling. We had seen this activity several times in the mother leopard, in particular two weeks before the latest mating when she walked a distance of some five kilometres along the roads, calling every few minutes, stopping to sniff the ground and rolling and frequently rubbing her body on the ground. This behaviour continued from seven o'clock to 10 o'clock at night and probably even after we left the area. Could this have signified the onset of the oestrus cycle that had led to the latest mating? The complicated question of these cycles was an intriguing one that we knew could be answered only by conducting detailed physiological tests on the leopards, a means that we unfortunately did not have.

Early one morning in May, we were following the young female leopard near Rhino Dam on the southern edge of the mother's territory. Her behaviour was typical of a leopard on the hunt. She walked slowly but purposefully, stopping every few metres to search the landscape ahead, tail twitching, ears forward, listening carefully before moving on again. Every now and then she would leap up into a tree or on to a termite mound to get a better view of her surroundings. At first it seemed to us that she was well fed and would not really need to hunt. But as we watched her we realized from the determined way in which she was hunting that she was in fact very hungry and that it was not a full belly we were looking at but a pregnant one.

Once again she showed some aggressive behaviour towards the Land Rovers, so ensuring that we all kept our distance. We

Portrait of African hawk eagle.

followed her for about an hour and during that time she did not stop once to rest but unremittingly continued searching for prey. Eventually she arrived at a waterhole and quenched her thirst, her bright pink tongue contrasting strongly with the dark water as she lapped. When we finally left her that morning, she still had not succeeded in finding any prey.

We saw her again at the end of June 1984. Once more she was hunting but this time she had a herd of impala in her sights. She was in a dense patch of scented thorn next to Hobbit's Hole clearing and she was using every available patch of cover to get close to the impala. We parked a short distance from her and watched as she stalked towards the herd. Every now and then she would stop and look at the impala, observe the way they were moving and then make an attempt to cut them off. Eventually she must have thought she was close enough and gave chase. But the impala were too quick and, giving their sharp alarm calls, scattered with leaps and bounds into the bush. The leopard then circled around in the direction that the impala had taken and made another attempt, once again without success.

As she settled down to rest beneath a thorn tree, we heard another leopard call from close by. The young female's reaction was immediate. She sat up, looked in the direction of the call, walked forward a few metres, scraped her hind legs vigorously on the ground and then turned at right-angles to the sound of the call. She continued walking, but stopped every few metres to scent-mark against bushes. Pete Arnot, who was in the second Land Rover, went off to find the leopard that had called and found the mother not more than 200 metres from her daughter. She was walking in the opposite direction.

This was an interesting interaction which suggested to us that the two leopards were at or near the boundaries of their respective territories, as neither of them showed any inclination to go after the other. Territorial behaviour seems designed to reduce the possibilities of physical clashes between individuals, a theory that this interaction illustrated quite clearly. Once an animal has established a territory, it advertises the fact by means of calls, scraping and scent-marking, signs that are usually respected by intruders. It is only when an individual somehow senses that it will be able to challenge the tenant of the territory, that the intruder will ignore these signs.

It was at about this time that we confirmed, from maps of all our leopard sightings, that the mother leopard had indeed shifted her activity into the northernmost part of her territory and that she was now spending less time around the Mshabene. Could it be that the presence of the young female so close to the south of her territory was pushing her further north? It seemed to be more than merely a coincidence that, just when the young female had become established in her territory around the Tugwaan, the mother should make a northerly shift.

But what interested us most about this interaction was the fact that the two leopards involved were mother and daughter. Did the mother leopard still recognize her offspring or did she see her as just another leopard which was competing for the same resources? Patterns of dispersal of young leopards from their mothers' territories were unknown, but here we had an example of a daughter who was living in a territory adjacent to her mother's. Could this possibly be more tolerable to the mother than having an unrelated leopard there? We hoped to obtain an answer to this question by watching the dispersal of the mother's other offspring.

Early on the morning of 18 July 1984, Warren came across the young female leopard walking purposefully southwards from Rhino Dam along Inky Thomas's Road and towards the pile of granite boulders where she had been born three years previously. As she approached the boulders, she stopped and gave a single low call before leaping up on to the top of the rocks and slipping into the crevice where we had seen the mother disappearing three years before. There could be only two reasons for this behaviour: either she had cubs in the rocks, or she was investigating suitable places to give birth.

We had all learnt to be very wary of the young female's aggressive nature and Warren parked his Land Rover some distance from the boulders, hoping he was near enough to hear the cubs. Even so, the leopard emerged once, threatened Warren's vehicle and then returned to the crevice. Warren waited patiently and eventually heard the unmistakable chirps of the cubs from within the granite. Another generation of cubs had been born!

I managed to reach the granite boulders only later that morning and I waited for a full hour, hoping to see or hear something of the cubs. As I sat there, a herd of buffalo came grazing over the crest of land above the rocks. They approached steadily closer until eventually the entire herd of about 300 was grazing around the boulders. I was reminded of the occasion when the young female was chased by the buffalo and I thought of her lying quietly with her cubs in the crevice as the nearest buffalo grazed no more than a metre away. The herd must have picked up the scent of the leopards, for they suddenly lifted their heads, snorted and stampeded back up the hill.

That night we visited the boulders again, and this time we could pick out the young mother in the light of the spotlights as she lay on her side within the crevice. We could not see the cubs but, after a few minutes, the young female came out of the rocks and headed into the darkness. In great anticipation, we drove closer and shone the lights into the gap in the rocks. There, cuddled next to each other, ears crumpled, their spots so close that they looked grey, were two tiny leopard cubs.

What intrigued us about this discovery was why, with numerous suitable places to choose from, the young female had given

A leopard in a tree. Photographers and artists often choose to depict leopards in this sort of situation, but in fact the animals spend only a small part of their lives in trees.

birth to her own cubs in the very spot where she herself had been born. Was there some sort of attachment to her natal lair or was her choice simply a coincidence? She remained in the boulders for another three days during which we got two or three sightings of the little cubs, their half-open eyes suggesting that they were no older than two weeks. On the fourth day we found tracks of the leopard going back and forth between the rocks and a termite mound 50 metres away in dense *Acacia schweinfurthii* on the bank of a donga. We found the female lying beneath the *Acacia* next to an opening in the mound and spent the rest of the morning watching from a distance as she first suckled and then groomed her little cubs.

They were the smallest that we had ever observed for any length of time and it was wonderful to see how their young mother – by this time only three years old – so gently took care of them. Once she got up and moved a short distance from the mound to defecate. While she was away, one of the little cubs stumbled from the safety of the hole and began to slide down the side of the mound towards the bottom of the donga. It cried in distress and the mother quickly returned, giving it a reassuring call. Then she picked it up and brought it carefully back to the safety of the termite mound.

The next day we returned to the lair to find that the vegetation at the opening to the termite mound had been trampled. There was no sign of the leopards but we could see a confusion of tracks in the soil. We were a little too far away to identify them and we did not want to get closer in case the leopard was still lying in the thicket somewhere, but we suspected from the heaviness of the prints that they did not belong to her.

Then we heard the alarm calls of vervet monkeys some distance to the south of the mound. We drove to the area from which they came and found tracks of a female leopard in the road. After following them for some time we eventually found the young mother walking back towards the termite mound giving the cub call every few seconds. When she reached the lair, she investigated the opening carefully and then walked around the mound several times, calling continually and interspersing the cub call with repeated grunting. Eventually she lay down on top of the mound.

Obviously the cubs were no longer around. About an hour later, when the leopard eventually left the lair, we checked the ground around the mound and found it covered in hyaena tracks. During the night the leopard had obviously left the lair to go hunting and the hyaena had found the cubs unattended. They were still very small, so it would not have taken the hyaenas long to finish them off. We found no sign of any remains at all.

As far as we knew, this was the young female's first litter and we wondered whether this tragic loss had anything to do with inexperience on her part. We had already seen the mother leopard successfully raise five cubs out of a possible seven and she had never lost any at such an early age, so we thought that possibly experience played a role in the selection of suitable lair sites that were safe from all predators.

We did not see the young female after this incident until one night at the end of August when we found her feeding on a freshly killed adult impala. She had not hoisted the kill as yet and, as we watched her, we heard the alarm snorts of impala not more than 100 metres away. Minutes later, three lionesses appeared out of the darkness on the track close to the Land Rover. They must have smelt the kill, for they were heading straight for the leopard, but she was alert and, seeing the lionesses approaching, grabbed the impala by the neck and tried to leap into a leadwood tree. She had only just started feeding on the kill when the lionesses arrived and had not yet been able to remove the stomach, so the carcass was still very heavy. The leopard managed to clamber half way up the tree trunk, only to be dragged down by the weight of the impala. She made two more attempts, but the kill was too heavy for her and, with time running out, she dropped it and leapt to the top of the tree just as the lionesses reached it. She watched from the safety of her perch as the lionesses, with much growling, quickly consumed the carcass.

After that we lost track of the young female for a few months, though we did get an occasional sighting of her in the Tugwaan area. Early in 1985 we saw her once and we thought that she was pregnant, but when we came across her again in April she showed no sign of either pregnancy or lactation. There were no further sightings of her for the next few months and we wondered what had become of her.

LEFT: *Leopards hoist their kills into trees to keep them out of reach of predators, especially lion and hyaena. Here the mother leopard snarls while feeding on an impala.*
OVERLEAF: *Aggression from the mother leopard as she rebuffs her 13-month-old daughter. This intolerance of female leopards towards their cubs increases as the cubs grow older. Eventually, the mother deserts them at about 13 months.*

Adult warthogs, with their formidably sharp, recurved tusks, are extremely brave animals and will charge at a leopard without hesitation. On this occasion, the leopard caught a piglet, only to be attacked by the mother warthog. Managing to leap up into the fork of a marula tree without dropping it, the leopard swiftly killed the squealing hog with a bite to the throat.

With graceful movements and using her tail for balance, a female leopard walks down the trunk
of a bent marula tree to begin her evening hunt. Knowing that leopards do most of their hunting at night, we were
surprised to discover how active they are when it is light – we have even found them hunting
in the middle of a hot summer day.

ABOVE: *Ears alert, eyes glaring and nose visible, a young male leopard peers over the top of a fallen dead tree trunk. Leopards use a combination of all three senses during the hunt, listening for calls or movements in the grass, using vantage points to watch for potential prey and sniffing the air or following scents along the ground.*
RIGHT: *With his bad eye furthest from the camera, the large scar-faced male peers over his shoulder late one night.*

Her tail raised, a female leopard completes her scent-marking ritual by squirting urine against a tree trunk. Both male and female leopards are territorial, the males appearing to have areas encompassing two or three female territories. If the territorial signs of scent-marking are ignored, leopards will eventually resort to physical clashes to resolve ownership.

*Hardly two months old, a leopard cub stares quizzically from the safety of a thicket
as its mother protectively crouches low. Female leopards are at their most dangerous when they have
young cubs such as this to protect and any approaches to lair sites have to
be made with the utmost caution.*

HUNTING

The impala were completely unaware of the presence of the leopard. There were about 90 grazing peacefully on either side of the track in the middle of Plaque Clearing, their tails and ears flicking at intervals. The grass was long and the leopard had been able to crawl undetected along the track until she was almost between the two groups of impala. Now she waited. She was in an ideal position. In order for the impala on one side of the track to join those on the other, they would have to cross almost precisely where she was crouched. Slowly, the impala on the eastern side began to move away from the track, leaving the other group behind.

The leopard lay in the track, body against the ground, head lifted so that she could peek over the grass at the impala, her ears flat. For a long time, the second group of impala milled about as they grazed, not moving any closer. But the leopard waited until at last the herd, realizing that they were being left behind, began to trot towards the track.

From our position in the Land Rover, it seemed that they were going to run straight into the leopard and we braced ourselves for the kill. In single file the impala came on and, one by one, they trotted across the road no more than two metres from the leopard. We waited with bated breath as first five, then 10, then 20 impala passed her, but still the leopard waited. We could not believe what we were seeing. For some reason, the leopard never made her final leap and when the last impala had crossed the road she sat up and slunk off after them.

We were to witness this type of behaviour again and again as we followed the leopards when they went on their hunts. With infinite patience, a leopard would spend as much as an hour stalking a single group of animals, watching them, anticipating their movements, circling around to cut them off, always waiting for exactly the right moment before finally leaping. Often, to our eyes, it seemed that the leopard was in a position to make the final pounce, but we began to realise that what appeared to be perfect to us was not perfect to the leopard. She always seemed to wait for exactly the right moment, rushing at the prey only when there was a near 100 per cent chance of catching it. As a result, we very seldom saw the leopard miss her prey once she had decided to charge.

Before we got to know the leopards, we had always understood them to be strictly nocturnal, hunting exclusively at night and then finding a dense thicket or tree in which to hide and rest during daylight hours. But once we began to follow the mother and her offspring, we realized that they are far more active during the day than we had previously imagined. We have witnessed them hunting not only at all hours of the night but also in the middle of the day. They certainly seem to do more hunting at night, but it is common to see a leopard hunting at 11 o'clock in the morning or at two o'clock in the afternoon, even on a hot summer day.

When hunting, a leopard will use a combination of eyesight, hearing and smell to detect the prey. The hunt is interrupted by many pauses when the leopard will sit on its haunches, sniff the air and simply listen quietly, or climb a tree on the edge of an open area to get a better view of the ground ahead. Hearing is perhaps the most important sense: we have often seen a leopard react to a variety of sounds, ranging from impala alarm calls to faint rustles in the grass, when the prey is nowhere visible. Vegetation-covered termite mounds serve as ideal resting places during the hunt as they provide the leopard with cover as well as a good view of the surrounding landscape. We have on several occasions seen a leopard sit up on its haunches and then lift its front legs off the ground, like a dog begging, in an attempt to see its prey over the long grass. We have also observed leopards

LEFT: *A female leopard prepares to drag a recently killed impala into cover.*
After making a kill, leopards will invariably drag the carcass out of sight of vultures
or to the foot of a tree to be hoisted later.

detecting their prey by making use of scent trails like hounds following the trail of a fox.

Once the prey has been spotted, the leopard's next task is to stalk as close to it as possible without being detected. This is not easy. A herd of impala is really a collection of eyes, ears and noses all programmed to detect predators such as leopards, and when one is trying to stalk 100 pairs of sense organs, the chances of being spotted are very high indeed. Nevertheless, the leopard accomplishes the kill time and again, using its camouflage and incredible patience. It watches the group of animals for long periods, works out the direction in which they are moving and then circles around until it is in the path that they are about to take. If the animals change direction for some reason, the leopard laboriously repeats the process. Once in the animals' path it lies in ambush, pouncing only when it is certain that it will succeed.

Warthog and redbilled oxpeckers.

This is the classic leopard hunt, but we have seen them use a number of other techniques. Once we were following a young female that was obviously hunting when she spotted a herd of impala in a clearing 100 metres in front of her. She stalked slowly across the clearing straight towards the herd, not using any cover at all. As soon as the impala spotted her, they turned and bounded away but the leopard, reacting like a cheetah, ran in a straight line towards them. She followed the impala across the clearing until they came to a wall of bush at one end and there they scattered, some disappearing into the thicket, others, disturbed by the obstacle, turning back in the direction of the leopard. Anticipating brilliantly, the leopard caught one of the impala in the open, killed it, and dragged it into a thicket to feed.

Although the phenomenon has been witnessed and written about in other parts of Africa, we have never seen a leopard leap out of a tree directly on to its prey. It is possible that in places such as East Africa, where there are far fewer trees, there is a much greater chance of an animal in its quest for shade finding its way to a tree concealing a leopard, but because the woodland at Londolozi is very dense, the chances that this will happen are very slim indeed. This is not to say that a Londolozi leopard will not leap out of a tree on to prey if the opportunity presents itself.

When hunting warthogs, leopards will employ the classic stalk-and-pounce method, but they will also attempt to catch them when they are entering or leaving their burrows in termite mounds. A hunting leopard will check most mounds that she comes across, sniffing at the entrance before moving on. If she detects the presence of an animal there, she will usually lie down just above the opening on the off chance that the warthog will come running out. We have never seen an experienced leopard actually go down into the burrow unless it was certain that the adult female warthog with her formidable tusks was not there, but we have seen young leopards disappear into the mound and sometimes successfully emerge with a baby warthog.

The leopard captures its prey by leaping up and grabbing at the animal with its front paws, at the same time biting into the neck. The ideal killing bite seems to be one to the throat, the leopard holding on to the kicking prey until it dies. But there have been times when we have seen the leopard bite the prey awkwardly at the back of the head or at the side of the neck and when this happens death usually takes a little longer. Sometimes, especially with smaller prey, this type of bite seems to be deliberate.

What is the leopard's favourite prey? As this is a question that we are frequently asked, we have kept a record of kills and at present this list includes all those found by us over the period from June 1982 until October 1988. During the course of that time the leopards killed over 400 animals. More than half of these were impala, the most abundant large mammal at Londolozi. Another common antelope species, the duiker, ranked second and the brave and ugly warthog third. Monkeys, bushbuck and hares were also often included in the leopards' diet. Of the 24 different species of animals killed by the leopards, 20 were mammals; two, the rock monitor and the leopard tortoise, were reptiles and two were birds – one francolin species and, strangely, a redbilled woodhoopoe.

When we analysed the list of kills and compared it with the numbers of animals occurring at Londolozi it was apparent that the leopard is very much an opportunistic hunter, tackling whatever it comes across during its hunt. In fact, the only factor that seems to limit the leopards' choice of prey is size. Adult animals of the six most commonly killed species, which together make up nearly 90 per cent of all the kills made, all weigh less than 50 kilograms. Large prey species, such as wildebeest, zebra and kudu, were consistently ignored during the hunt. Of course, bravery and aggression on the part of a prey animal, such as the warthog, also played a part in making the leopard decide against taking certain animals, as we saw on a number of occasions.

Once the leopard has made the kill its troubles are not over, for it then has to contend with scavengers such as hyaenas, lions, vultures and even small mammals such as mongoose and genets. The most serious competitor for the leopard's kill is the spotted hyaena, a large predator with powerful shoulders and weak-looking hind legs, that survives in the Londolozi area mainly by scavenging meat from other predators. It is bigger and stronger than the leopard from which it easily steals kills, but the leopard is able to avoid this competition to a certain extent by hoisting its victims into trees safely out of the hyaena's reach.

A clash between these two predators led to one of the most interesting interactions between leopard and hyaena that we had ever witnessed and also afforded us our best view of the dominant male leopard.

At the end of August 1984, shortly after the mother leopard had taken her cubs to a kill for the first time, we found her hunting through a patch of *Combretum* woodland in the northern part of her territory. She spotted a herd of impala and we lost sight of her as she disappeared in pursuit of them. We switched off the Land Rover's engine to listen and immediately heard the sharp grunt of an impala being caught. Straight away, we drove through the bush in the direction of the sound and found the leopard throttling an adult female impala on the edge of an open clearing. A passing hyaena must have heard the noise as well for it was at the kill almost before the leopard had completed it. It circled warily around for a while and then, throwing caution to the wind, trotted straight to where the leopard was lying with the impala. The hyaena grabbed the dead animal's hind-quarters and pulled, but the leopard hung on to the other end and a tug-of-war ensued, the impala being lifted off the ground as the two predators tugged at it from opposite directions. Then suddenly the hyaena released its hold and trotted off into the woodland.

Cheetah portrait.

The leopard looked up at the departing hyaena, then knelt down and quickly began to feed. After devouring some of the meat from between the back legs, she dragged the carcass to the foot of a marula tree where she fed on it for a little longer. Then suddenly she grabbed her kill by the neck and with a single leap, hoisted it into the tree, wedging it into a fork about 10 metres up. The impala was almost completely intact and weighed as much as the leopard, so it was an amazing feat that we had just witnessed. In most cases, a leopard will feed off the kill for some time, usually removing the stomach before hoisting it. In this instance, the presence of the hyaena must have pushed her into hoisting sooner.

A few minutes later, the hyaena returned to the base of the marula. Agitated, the leopard attempted to hoist the impala higher, but the carcass proved too heavy for her and as she tried to leap higher, she fell on to a lower branch, the full weight of the kill hanging from her teeth. There was no suitable place in which she could wedge it and we watched from the Land Rover as she struggled for the next hour to manoeuvre it into a suitable position. We found the process almost unbearable to watch. Whenever the leopard gathered enough strength to make another attempt, the impala's leg would get hooked on a branch and she would have to rest again for some minutes. Meanwhile, the hyaena patiently lay beneath the tree, waiting for the inevitable. Finally, however, the leopard gathered together all her strength and, with a single do-or-die leap, managed to wedge the impala in a branch a metre higher up the tree. The hyaena would have to wait a little longer.

As the leopard sat in the branches panting over the kill, we noticed that her lower left canine tooth had been broken down to the root. We had not noticed the injury before so it must have occurred recently. She may even have broken the tooth in her efforts to hoist the impala and we wondered whether this would in any way affect her ability to kill and hoist in future.

After resting for some time, the leopard climbed down and carefully began to scrape grass and sand over the drag-mark and scraps of carcass that were on the ground, paying particular attention to the area at the base of the tree. We had seen leopards do this many times before and we suspected that it was an attempt to hide scent trails that scavengers could otherwise follow. When she had completed her chore she left the area, presumably to fetch the cubs.

We returned to the area later in the morning to find that the kill had been moved on to the top of a termite mound a few metres from the tree. There was no sign of the leopard at first, but shortly after our arrival the mother arrived at the kill with her cubs and began to feed. When she had finished, she carefully scraped leaves and sand around the kill, called the cubs and together they moved off through the woodland in a south-westerly direction.

As they moved away, we were surprised to see a large male leopard advancing towards the family. This was the first time we had actually seen a male together with the mother and cubs and we wondered how she would react. The male ambled towards them and when he reached the mother the two adult leopards greeted each other by rubbing faces together in much the way that lions do. Together, the male, the female and the cubs strolled westwards into the woodland.

Here, for the first time, was definite proof that a male leopard will amicably join up with his family. That night we saw more of this unusual interaction. Warren returned to the site of the kill to find that the carcass had been dragged away. With Kimbian, he followed the drag-mark which stretched for an unusually long distance until they found the kill stashed in a weeping boer-bean tree at the bottom of a donga about a kilometre away. There was no sign of the leopards.

Later that night, Pete Anderson returned to the kill to discover that all four of the leopards were in the tree and a hungry hyaena was waiting on the ground below. The leopards took it in turns to feed off the kill and all the time that they were together they showed no aggression whatever towards one another. Pete got a good look at the male for the first time that night. It was the large animal with the scarred eye that Warren had seen so many months before.

We watched the four leopards for another day as they finished feeding on the meat. Two hyaenas spent most of the time waiting patiently below the tree, snatching the odd scrap that dropped as the leopards fed. At one time the entire rib-cage fell out of the tree, nearly landing on top of one of the hyaenas and frightening them both away. A few minutes later they returned and polished off the rib-cage, their patience finally rewarded.

PREVIOUS SPREAD: *The mother leopard stands frozen in mid-stride, a picture of intense concentration as she stares fixedly in the direction of a rustling she has heard in the long grass ahead of her.*
ABOVE: *As leopard cubs grow older, they become more adventurous and increasingly inquisitive, stalking anything that moves, even animals as large as buffalo or elephant. Here a young male leopard stalks a buffalo bull weighing over 900 kg.*

The male leopard was still very wary of the Land Rovers and we only had really good views of him at night provided we sat quietly and were patient. We got one good sighting of him on the last evening the leopards were at the kill. The female and the cubs were all in the tree and the male signified his presence by some low growling from the bottom of the donga as he encountered the hyaenas. We sat in the darkness with our Land Rover parked next to the tree and waited for him. Eventually we heard the scraping as he leapt into the branches and we waited a few more minutes until we heard him beginning to feed. Then we switched on the spotlights to reveal him in all his splendour, his magnificent spotted coat glowing and his ugly face staring towards us every so often.

This was the first time I had had a good view of a large male leopard from close up and it was truly an awe-inspiring sight. As he fed on the kill no more than two metres from the mother leopard, we got a very good idea of exactly how large he was. He certainly seemed to be at least twice the size of the mother and what impressed me most was the thickness of his neck and the flap of skin like a dewlap hanging below it. We watched until he finished feeding; then he climbed down from the tree and disappeared into the darkness. Next morning we found his tracks heading west along the main road. His social call was over.

'Leopards will kill just for the sake of killing.' This is a statement that we have heard many times, especially from farmers who have had the distressing experience of finding a dozen sheep slaughtered by a leopard that had entered a pen during the night. Indeed, we have often come across leopards in the wilds which have made more than one kill in the space of a few hours, despite the fact that they already had full stomachs. And there is a scene in Alan Root's classic film *The Year of the Wildebeest* that shows a leopard resting among branches with no fewer than four wildebeest calves that he has hoisted into the trees around him.

To catch and kill a prey animal is not an easy task for a leopard and so when the opportunity presents itself it will not hesitate to kill, even if it already has some food. The carcass is never wasted as the leopard, not being averse to rotten meat, will simply store it in a tree and return to it once the first kill has been eaten. Of course, when confronted by an unnatural situation such as a pen full of sheep, the leopard will just go on killing one animal after another.

One afternoon in September 1984 we witnessed an example of this opportunistic behaviour by the mother leopard. She had left her cubs in a donga near the Mshabene and had moved northwards from there to hunt. In the woodland to the west of our airstrip, where we found her in the early afternoon, she spotted a family of warthogs, a female and three youngsters, grazing quietly near a termite mound. Seeing the closeness of the mound, the leopard circled around until it was between her and the hogs and then, using it as cover, she stalked closer and closer to the unsuspecting creatures.

When she reached the mound, she very slowly moved around the edge, keeping her body and her ears flat until she could see the hogs. They were moving slowly towards the mound and all the leopard had to do was wait. Steadily they came closer until eventually the leopard pounced, catching one of the youngsters in a squealing cloud of dust. But the mother warthog was not going to let her offspring go so easily and she charged at the leopard causing her to drop the hog briefly. Somehow, the leopard caught it again and managed to throttle it with a bite to the throat which took some time. She dragged the kill into a thicket, fed off it for a while and then rested and groomed herself. As the sun began to set, she got up and started heading in the direction of the lair where she had left the cubs. However, she had not gone far when she spotted a duiker rubbing its facial glands against some bushes and quite oblivious of her presence. The leopard crouched down and, using the dense bush as cover, stalked in a straight line towards the duiker. At the last minute the duiker spotted the leopard and turned to run, but it was too late. The leopard already had her paws on it and it began to bleat plaintively. She bit the kicking, squealing animal on the nape of the neck until at last it succumbed. As darkness fell, the leopard dragged the kill up into a marula tree and then set off again towards the cubs.

She brought them to the tree holding the duiker kill first, and they spent the night and the next morning feeding on it. We wondered if she had forgotten about the warthog, but the following afternoon she took the cubs to its carcass on which they fed over the next three days.

We saw another example of this ability to remember a few weeks later when she killed a monkey about two kilometres from the cubs and, on her way back to them, killed an adult impala only 50 metres from where they were. They spent three days feeding on the impala and we were certain that after this time she would have forgotten about a small kill like a monkey. However, when she left the impala, she took the cubs directly through the bush to the monkey.

■   ■   ■

How did the cubs learn their hunting skills? We had already seen that the leopards' hunting technique is acquired through experience more than anything else, the inquisitive nature of the youngsters ensuring that they will stalk and chase any little thing that they come across.

One day the mother leopard was moving through the bush with her offspring when the male cub spotted a rock monitor on the ground. He immediately chased after it and it slithered up into a knob-thorn tree. There the cub attempted to hit it with his paws, but the monitor, keeping its back to the leopard, repeatedly whipped at him with its tail, sending the leopard backwards in fright each time it did so. Whenever the leopard backed off, the monitor climbed higher into the tree until it climbed to the end of a rather thin branch. Cornered now, the lizard turned to face its tormentor, expanding its neck in a threat display and opening its mouth whenever the leopard came close. Gingerly, the cub stretched out a tentative paw, only to have it bitten. After a few minutes of this treatment, the male cub left the monitor and the female cub came up into the tree. She was much more cautious, tapped at the lizard two or three times and then left it. Soon the male, finding the monitor irresistible, climbed back into the tree and, snarling aggressively, tried to catch it with his paws. But the monitor held its own and eventually the cub abandoned it.

The rock monitor has another means of defence. One night a young male leopard, attracted by a rustling sound, pounced into a dense patch of grass and came up with a monitor in his mouth. He settled down in the long grass and we heard what sounded like the crunching of bones. After a few minutes the leopard went back into the thicket and came up with a second monitor which it also proceeded to chew on. Eventually the leopard left the area and we got out of the Land Rover to have a closer look at what we thought would be the remains of the monitors. To our surprise, we found both lizards lying in the grass completely intact. Presuming that they were dead, I picked one up to show it to my guests. As we studied it, I suddenly realised that its eyes were open and that they were swivelling in their sockets, having a good look at me. The monitors were playing dead!

Over the years we have seen the cubs stalk and chase all manner of things. They have entertained themselves for minutes on end with fluttering moths; they have caught tortoises on the ground and they have chased after starlings in the highest branches of the tallest trees. They regularly corner mongoose in hollow logs and termite mounds and we have watched as they try to deal with strange animals such as pangolins and porcupines. All of this is largely a kind of play activity that eventually leads to the leopards' becoming more and more expert at stalking, catching and dealing with various animals.

The cubs probably begin learning from the mother from the age of two months when she starts to lead them to kills. Very often, while moving from lair to kill, the mother will come across prey and will stalk it in full view of the cubs. In this way they probably learn some of their hunting techniques, at first simply by watching as the mother hunts but, as they get older, by actively stalking the prey as well.

More often than not, this results in the cub botching the kill for the mother, but on one occasion the participation of the male cub actually assisted her. While moving with the cubs one morning, she spotted a herd of impala and, leaving the cubs behind, stalked after them. When she had disappeared behind some bushes, the male cub proceeded to stalk the herd, awkwardly slinking across the clearing towards them. It was not long before the impala saw him and they stood staring at him with ears cocked forward for a few minutes, all the while giving their alarm snorts. Then they turned away and ran towards the bush into which the mother had disappeared minutes earlier. As they vanished into the thickets we heard the grunt of an impala being

Yellowbilled kite in flight.

caught. Unwittingly, the cub had helped the mother make a kill by chasing the antelope towards her.

Cheetah teach their cubs to kill by catching an animal, maiming it and then releasing it for the cubs to deal with. It is a cruel method and unpleasant to watch as the inexperienced cubs usually take a long time to pull down the unfortunate victim, sometimes so long that the mother loses patience and finally kills the animal herself. We had seen lions behave in a similar way and we had read about this 'motherly tuition' in leopards as well, but we had not as yet witnessed it.

■ ■ ■

At the end of December 1984 we had the opportunity to watch a classic leopard hunt from beginning to end when we found the mother stalking impala in a patch of magic guarri on the western edge of her territory. She watched the herd and then, seeing the direction in which they were moving, circled around to cut them off. But as she crossed a gap between two bushes, the impala saw her, gave their alarm snorts and then trotted southwards through a thicket towards the main road.

Seeing them move off, the leopard first ran westwards away from them and then, once she was out of sight, turned southwards on to the main road and, using its verge as cover, crawled quickly eastwards towards the point where she anticipated they would cross.

She waited in the road just as a group of eight impala came out of the woodland heading straight towards her. But she had slightly misjudged her position and, when she noticed that they were going to cross the road some 10 metres behind her, she quickly crawled back, still using the verge as cover, until she was directly in their path. She lay there, her skin quivering, her hind legs tucked up under her body, ready to pounce. As the first impala reached the verge, the leopard sprang, catching it with her forepaws and biting it in the back of the neck as it tried to break away. But she had not caught it properly, and the kicking impala leapt some 10 metres away before the leopard managed to grasp and hold it. The two animals stood locked together like a statue for at least five minutes before the impala slowly began to sink to its knees.

We had witnessed a classic hunt. A little over an hour had passed from the moment the mother leopard initially spotted the impala until the kill and in this time we had seen her stalk, anticipate, be spotted, circle around and anticipate again, and then finally leap up and make the kill. It was wonderful to be able to watch all her inbred skills – her patience, her determination, her slyness and her quickness – as they finally come together in a successful hunt.

■ ■ ■

Over the next few months the mother leopard continued to raise her litter. There were several interactions with hyaenas, but nothing life-threatening and the cubs continued to thrive. The male made his first kill, a dwarf mongoose, at the end of March 1985 when he was 11 months old and a week later the female cub killed a rock monitor. Shortly after this, a clash occurred with the young female who had wandered into the mother's territory.

The mother had killed an impala which she had hoisted into a tree prior to fetching the cubs but when they arrived there they found the young female feeding on the carcass. We wondered what would happen and we were amazed to see the female cub, only about 11 months old, aggressively approach the tree, baring her teeth in a throaty snarl. The young female snarled back at the cub, and the two leopards stared at each other, hissing loudly. This stand-off lasted at least 10 minutes and then, suddenly, with a loud growl, the cub rushed aggressively at the young female, springing into the tree to get at her. Obviously taken aback, the young female responded by leaping from a height of about seven metres straight on to the ground below. As she hit it, the mother leopard, who had been watching the proceedings, rushed forward and nipped the young female at the base of the tail just as she turned and bounded off.

We were most surprised to see the cub react so aggressively to the presence of a strange adult leopard. The young female, being much larger and also having the advantage of a higher position in the tree, could have dealt with the cub very easily. The only explanation we could think of was that the young female knew that she was intruding and as a result had acted submissively. The next day we found the mother in the same area calling and scent-marking continually and we suspected that this was a reaction to the intrusion.

We had no further sightings of the young female over the next few months and during that time the mother successfully guided her cubs to independence, eventually deserting them in July, when they were about 15 months old.

■   ■   ■

Two months later, we noticed that she was pregnant and lactating heavily and in October 1985 she gave birth to her fifth litter of cubs. The three months that had passed since the independence of the fourth litter had gone so quickly that we wondered how much time the mother leopard actually had to herself. We looked back over our records and were amazed to see that she had spent nearly 80 per cent of her time caring for cubs and that a large proportion of the remaining time had been spent in a state of pregnancy.

The young female, meanwhile, had reappeared. In September 1985 she was found walking along the Tugwaan investigating a

African wild dogs on an impala kill.

number of large granite boulders that seemed an ideal place in which to give birth to cubs. We could see that she was heavily pregnant and lactating as well, indicating that the birth was imminent. But, after spending some time at the boulders, she left them and continued southwards.

A month later we found the young female again, and this time we could see that she was no longer pregnant although she was definitely still lactating. We wondered where she had left her cubs but unfortunately we were unable to follow her as she disappeared into heavy bush country.

However, Carlson and I were determined to find the litter and the next morning we were out with our willing guests well before sunrise and searching for the young female's tracks. Carlson's sharp eyes picked them up as soon as we got into a rocky part of the Tugwaan where it was crossed by the road. Carlson guided us as the tracks led eastwards, every so often pointing out a faint paw-print on the hard ground. After about a kilometre, the tracks turned southwards through the bush. Here the tracks were more difficult to follow and Carlson had to leave the Land Rover periodically to check the ground on foot. He would examine the direction of the last paw-print and then quickly walk on ahead until he picked up another. I once asked him how he knew which way to go once he had lost a track and his answer was simplicity itself. Just pretend that you are a leopard and choose a path through the bush. I was amazed at how often he was right.

During these tracking episodes Carlson really came into his own. On the Land Rover he spoke very little, but as soon as we got on to tracks he began to share his knowledge with me, pointing out footprints invisible to me, showing me which fruits were edible and which plants were used for various purposes – the devil's thorn creeper, the leaves of which, when mixed with water, make a very useful soap that really works; the enormous tuber of *Boophane* containing a sap used as a fish poison; and a myriad other fascinating things. Walking through the bush with men like Carlson is an endless journey of discovery.

Eventually the tracks emerged on a road a kilometre or so to the south, but it was not long before they went back through a very dense patch of bush alongside the Tugwaan. Rather than follow the tracks, Carlson suggested that we should drive into the thick sand of the Tugwaan itself. This was a good move, for we had not gone more than 100 metres when Carlson suddenly waved at me to stop. In the sand, crossing directly through the Tugwaan on to the southern bank, were the leopard's tracks. As we looked down at them, we were suddenly aware that there was the smell of a dead animal in the air. Cautiously, I drove the Land Rover on to the southern bank of the donga towards the dense thickets growing there. We peered into the shadows of each patch of bush until Carlson suddenly clicked his fingers. In the direction in which he pointed, in the deepest part of the thicket,

LEFT: *While hunting, leopards will regularly use trees as vantage points from which to scan the landscape ahead for potential prey.*

ABOVE: *Often preyed on by leopard, the bushbuck, as its name implies, is an animal inhabiting the more densely vegetated areas.*

lay an impala carcass, its bloated white belly revealing its presence. We cautiously searched the area, but were unable to find any sign of the leopard.

That afternoon we returned to the kill and found the young female reclining languidly in the soft sand of the Tugwaan. She was lying on her side, and we could see quite clearly that her teats had recently been suckled as the soft white fur around them was matted with moisture. We spent the rest of the afternoon watching her, waiting for her to move, until eventually, at dusk, she stood up and began walking up the Tugwaan.

We followed in the increasing darkness, keeping our distance as the young female moved along the riverbed and then saw her turning on to the northern bank and into a dense thicket of scented thorn. We followed as best we could, ducking under the low branches and getting scratched here and there. Then she came out on to a road and continued westwards along it until she reached a point where it crossed the Tugwaan. There was some water in the riverbed and she stopped and took a long drink, her reflection beautifully lit up by the spotlights. Then she lay down beside the water and groomed herself, licking the fur on her belly and along her back and rubbing her paws over her face. From the direction of the kill came the whoop of a hyaena and upstream along the Tugwaan we could hear the quiet chirruping of a barred owl. Eventually the leopard stood up and headed northwards through the bush. Five hundred metres from the Tugwaan she disappeared into a small donga filled with a dense pile of dead brush.

From our position we were unable to follow her, so I manoeuvred the Land Rover around to the opposite bank of the donga, eventually managing to squeeze it between some small knob-thorn trees from where we had a reasonable view. But the donga was deep and it was impossible to see anything without going right to the edge. So we sat there quietly and listened and before long we heard the high-pitched calls of a cub.

Just then there was a sudden movement in the grass and Carlson yelled at me. By the time I got the rifle to my shoulder, the leopard was at the Land Rover, snarling, hissing and growling aggressively. Somehow I managed to convey to the guests that they should sit still and to shine both spotlights into her eyes. There was no door on my side of the Land Rover and the leopard was less than a metre from my exposed leg. At the end of the rifle those huge cold yellow eyes stared up at me, blinking in the brightness of the lights. All I had to do was pull the trigger of the .458 and the leopard would be dead, but the only words that kept circulating through my mind were: 'Don't come any closer. I don't want to shoot you, I don't want to shoot you!'

We sat transfixed for what seemed like ages, the leopard crouched, ready to pounce, the people in the Land Rover utterly silent. Every so often somebody would move slightly and the squeak of clothes against the vinyl of the seat caused the leopard's eyes to widen. I noticed with a cold shiver that my two-way radio was still turned up, and I prayed that no one would call us, for a sudden noise would have further provoked the leopard. At last, however, she got up, retreated a few metres and lay down again, facing the Land Rover. This was my chance and slowly and carefully I reached for the ignition switch and started the engine. The leopard did not react, and moving slowly I put the vehicle into reverse and gradually backed out.

The relief was indescribable. We all started laughing nervously and I suddenly noticed that my hands and knees were shaking uncontrollably. This was the closest I had ever been to shooting a leopard in self-defence and it was an experience that I wished never to repeat. The thought of those bared canine teeth and those ice-cold yellow eyes drilling into me is still enough to send shivers down my spine. What amazed me most was the reaction of the guests. We had always been taught that as they are new to this environment there is always a risk that they might panic in moments of danger. But my guests were remarkably cool and I feel sure that if it had not been for their calm reaction to the situation, the incident would have ended differently.

A young leopard chews on the skin of an impala carcass. Leopards always start feeding in the soft belly parts between the back legs and then work their way up the carcass. The ends of smaller bones such as the ribs are often chewed through, but the larger ones are generally left intact.

A hunting leopard pauses to peer into the bush ahead. During the hunt, a leopard will often stop to listen for potential prey or, once the prey has been spotted, to make certain which way the animals are going before moving to cut them off. Using infinite patience, it will spend an hour or longer stalking a single group of animals.

*Most leopard kills are quick, clean affairs involving very little struggling. Sometimes, however, the leopard can be a
fraction too slow: it catches the prey without a firm enough grip which results in the victim's frantic efforts to escape.
Here, in a flurry of dust and movement, a common duiker puts up a fight, only to succumb moments later.*

PREVIOUS SPREAD: *On the ground or in trees, leopards move with beautiful grace and agility. Here*
a slower shutter-speed catches a leopard in a blur of movement as it trots along a track in pursuit of prey.
LEFT: *Supremely confident in the higher branches of a marula tree in full foliage,*
a leopard leaps a distance of over three metres from one limb to another.
ABOVE: *Winter night scene of a contented leopard resting in a leafless marula tree, her common*
duiker kill draped over a branch and the tail of one of her cubs just visible. At Londolozi, duikers feature regularly
in the leopard's diet and, second only to impala, make up just over 12 per cent of all kills.

GAMES

There were now two litters of young leopard cubs to be viewed at Londolozi, one of which was the second generation descended from the mother. We looked forward with tremendous excitement to watching them grow up – but this was not to be.

The young female had one cub, but as we were now very wary of her we saw less of them than we would have liked. We did see her transferring the cub from the Nyatini area in October 1985 and we had three more sightings of the two of them together over the next four months. Then, in February 1986, a lioness killed the cub although it was about four months old and should have been able to climb trees without any problems. We never actually saw what happened but John and Elmon investigated the area afterwards and were able to deduce from the tracks that the lioness had been lying in ambush as the two leopards walked along a game path and had caught them totally unawares. Afterwards, the young female reacted very much as the mother leopard had done when she lost her two cubs to lions, feeding on her offspring, hoisting it into a tree and then spending a few days calling for it before eventually leaving the area.

We first saw the mother leopard's new litter in November 1985 when we followed her to a pile of granite boulders in a donga near the centre of her territory. She lay down on top of the rocks, gave the cub call two or three times and a pair of little cubs, less than two months old, stumbled unsteadily out of the boulders to greet her. She groomed them, licking lovingly over their soft fur as they settled down to suckle. As we watched her lying there, completely relaxed and no more than five metres from us, we realized what a special leopard she was. She obviously had an unusually placid nature, even allowing us to view her very small cubs, and in this revealed a nature contrasting strongly with that of every other leopard that we knew. Even her offspring, who had grown up with the Land Rovers, showed a

degree of unpredictability, but the mother leopard was unique.

At first there was not much to distinguish between the cubs but as they grew up their differing characters became more obvious, the female being fairly placid and the male developing into a robust and mischievous young leopard. Both were enormously inquisitive, stalking absolutely anything that moved.

When tracking the two cubs on foot, we saw this inquisitiveness lead to many amusing incidents. One of them was described by Paddy Hagelthorn, an ex-Zimbabwean who had recently joined us as a ranger.

'We were following the tracks of the mother leopard and her two cubs along a road,' he told us, 'when they turned into a large patch of *Combretum* woodland and disappeared. We checked all the roads in the vicinity and eventually found only the mother's tracks leaving the area. Obviously she had left the cubs behind so we returned to where we had last seen them and, leaving the Land Rover, my tracker, Dlaman, and I tried to follow the tracks on foot. It was not long before we lost them as the grass was very thick and the ground hard, but as we knew the cubs were in there somewhere, we kept searching, checking on likely spots such as thickets and termite mounds. After some time,' Paddy continued, 'we noticed the birds were giving their alarm calls just behind us. Thinking they were reacting to the presence of the leopards, we checked the bush where they were calling but found nothing. While we continued searching the bird calls persisted and although we checked again and again we found nothing.'

Assuming that their presence had disturbed the birds, Paddy and Dlaman decided to ignore the calls and eventually, after half an hour of searching, gave up and turned back to return to the car. 'There in front of us,' said Paddy, 'with a flock of white helmetshrikes fluttering and calling in the bush above him, was the male leopard cub. He had been stalking us all the time. We

A young male leopard, tongue lolling, yawns lazily as he looks towards the camera. Young leopards are extremely playful during their first two years, stalking, chasing, pouncing and investigating literally anything in their environment. This play activity is vital for the leopard's future survival as it is in this way that its hunting skills are honed.

decided to play his game and, pretending that we had not seen him, turned our backs on him and slowly walked away, every so often stealing a look over our shoulders. He was still following us and we allowed him to continue for some minutes before we returned to the Land Rover.'

Early one morning at the beginning of June, when the cubs were only eight months old, the male made his first kill. He and the mother had detected something in a bush and were in the process of stalking it. Losing patience, the cub suddenly rushed at the bush and disappeared into it. There was a loud high-pitched growling and he emerged with an adult civet dangling from his jaws. This was one of the earliest maiden kills we had seen from a cub and the fact that the victim was such a large animal – civets are omnivorous and weigh an average of 10 kilograms – made it all the more impressive.

The cub played with the carcass for hours, pouncing on it, throwing it in the air, running off with it and not allowing the other leopards to come close. Then they all moved down into a large donga system near the river, the male cub proudly carrying his trophy. There he made numerous attempts to hoist it into a fallen tree before finally dragging it into the bottom of the donga where he left it for the female cub to play with. Like skunks, civets have scent glands that give off a foul-smelling substance when they are disturbed and this specimen was no exception for there was a strong and pungent smell permeating the air. We suspected that this was why none of the leopards attempted to feed on the kill for, after playing with the carcass a little longer, the three leopards disappeared into the dense reeds in the riverbed leaving the carcass in the bottom of the donga.

This kill by the male must have spurred the cubs on, for between them they dispatched a monkey, a banded mongoose, a scrub hare and a francolin during the course of the next three weeks. The cubs from previous litters had made their first kills at between nine and 11 months, but these youngsters were still only eight months old.

At the beginning of July 1986 an interesting interaction occurred between the cubs and a group of warthogs. These amusingly ugly animals sleep by night in old antbear holes in termite mounds which, on clear sunny days, they leave very early in the morning. But when it is overcast, as was the case on this particular morning, the warthogs stay in the hole for longer.

Earlier, we had picked up the tracks of the mother and cubs heading north along our western boundary. The trackers had done a great job following them for the greater part of two kilometres until they eventually found the two cubs. They were stalking a small herd of impala but the impala soon saw the cubs and ran off leaving them to play their games. Just then the mother leopard called from nearby and the cubs bounded off to join her as she led them towards a termite mound with a freshly

Dwarf mongoose on the lookout.

used hole in it. A few metres from it, she lay down and just then a female warthog popped out her head. The mother leopard simply looked on as the warthog stood at the entrance for a few seconds, staring at the leopards before it suddenly ran off into the bush in a cloud of dust.

Confused by the sudden activity, the cubs merely sat there gazing towards the disappearing hog. Then a young warthog emerged from the hole and although this time the cubs gave chase, the grunting and squealing hog made good its escape. The cubs returned to the hole just as a third warthog popped its head out and, seeing the leopards, promptly reversed into the burrow. The cubs investigated the hole for a few minutes before their mother finally called them and led them away.

What interested us most about this interaction was the way the mother leopard seemed to lead the cubs to the hole and then leave them to make an attempt at catching the warthogs. This was the first time we had seen some suggestion of the 'motherly tuition' that we had read about.

Over the next few weeks the cubs entertained us immensely. One day they were left near Big Dam in a patch of bush where a large jackal-berry tree was in fruit. The deliciously sweet berries attracted a variety of birds: starlings, purplecrested and grey louries, orioles and green pigeons – a fluttering of feathers that the cubs could not resist. They scampered up into the tree and, climbing to the highest branches some 15 metres above the ground, they attempted to catch the birds. They leapt about in the shaking branches, completely ignoring the precariousness of their situation. Once or twice they slipped and fell on to a lower branch but somehow they managed to stay in the tree. They never caught a bird, but they certainly seemed to be having fun.

Three days later, we were watching the male cub playing in the Mshabene just below Big Dam when one of my guests accidentally dropped his camera case on the ground next to the Land Rover. Quick as a flash, the cub leapt on to it and carried it up into a fallen tree. There, he played a little game with it, dropping it, running down to pick it up, carrying it into the tree and then dropping it again. Every so often he would settle down and chew on it before continuing with the game until, after half an hour of fun, he tired of the artificial leather and left the now ragged camera case lying in the sand.

One night at the beginning of August, while the mother leopard was away hunting, the cubs came across a porcupine. Porcupines have specialized hollow quills in their tails which, when rattled together, make a loud noise. If a porcupine is cornered, it will raise its quills to form a prickly barrier and will then stamp its feet and rattle its tail in an attempt to frighten away the predator. If a leopard is to kill a porcupine, it has to get around to the unprotected front end and catch the animal by its face or under its throat before it has a chance to turn around.

Porcupines seem to know this and will usually bury their faces in a bush or against a tree trunk with nothing but their formidable quills protruding.

On this occasion the porcupine behaved typically: it thrust its head against a tree trunk and the cubs were uncertain what to do. Whenever one of the leopards gingerly stretched out a paw to touch the porcupine, it would suddenly make a loud noise and reverse rapidly in the direction of the leopard, pricking it sharply and startling it. When the cubs circled round to the front, the porcupine turned its back to them, keeping the barrier of spines between them. A quill broke off in the female cub's paw and she withdrew to try to remove it.

But the male cub persisted, stabbing at the porcupine with his paws, withdrawing as it responded and then rolling on to his back in frustration, dangerously exposing his eyes to the quills in the process. This sparring continued for at least an hour, the porcupine always keeping its back safely towards its attacker and the leopard becoming more and more frustrated. Eventually a quill stuck in the cub's foot and as he concentrated on trying to remove it with his teeth, the porcupine took advantage of his preoccupation and escaped, none the worse for wear apart from a few quills lost.

■ ■ ■

One afternoon in July 1986, we got our first sighting of the young female in over four months. She was moving through the Big Dam area very close to where the mother had recently left her cubs and she was scent-marking and rolling and scraping intensively. When she crouched down to drink at Big Dam we noticed that she was lactating heavily and that her teats had recently been utilized. This meant that she was feeding her third litter of cubs and we hoped that she would have better luck this time.

Two months later one of the rangers from a neighbouring property reported seeing a leopard with three cubs near our boundary in the area that the young female frequented. We hoped that it was she.

Meanwhile, it seemed that the mother had once again shifted her territory back to the core area of the Mshabene as this was where she now regularly left the cubs. While she was away, they continued with their games. One day in early September, while we were watching the female cub, she heard the sound of a herd of buffalo nearby and, inquisitive as usual, she followed up on it. Eventually she encountered the herd grazing peacefully in the woodland to the west of Big Dam and for a few minutes she stalked them quietly. Then some of the buffalo noticed her and immediately charged at her but she quickly leapt into a tree on top of a termite mound and looked down at them. However, the buffalo seemed determined to get at her; two or three of them came snorting towards her and, putting their front feet on top

Crested francolin threesome roosting.

of the mound, attempted to reach up to her. The tree in which the leopard cub was perched was not very big, but she climbed further up it until she was precariously balanced among the thinner branches, and not more than a metre above the probing noses of the buffalo. For some time they mingled beneath the tree, taking it in turns to climb up the mound and investigate the leopard.

After about 20 minutes the buffalo slowly started to move away and as they drifted off the leopard tried to scramble down the tree. However, the moment the herd saw the movement, they rushed back, sending the leopard clambering back to the tree top. This happened two or three times before the cub decided to run the gauntlet and, waiting for the moment when she considered the buffalo were sufficiently far away, she ran down the tree. Unfortunately for her, the buffalo saw her and in an enormous cloud of dust that obscured the cub from our view, stampeded after her. We hastily drove the Land Rover in the direction in which she had run off, bypassing the returning buffalo as we bumped along. Eventually, as the dust cleared, we saw her walking calmly back towards Big Dam, more enlightened now, but unscathed by her alarming experience.

A few days later we found the male cub investigating a gentle rustling in the grass. He had found a pangolin, a rare anteater and one of southern Africa's threatened mammals. This strange creature walks about slowly on its hindlegs, keeping its small front feet off the ground and using its long scale-covered tail as a support. Its sole means of protection is a layer of heavy scales that cover the upper half of its body, and, when danger threatens, it quickly rolls itself up into a ball, its face and soft underparts well protected by its armoured covering.

As soon as the leopard approached, the pangolin rolled up into its protective ball. The cub held it between his paws and tried to chew on it, but the scales were tough and sharp-edged, so he had to bite very carefully. Very soon he found the inanimate object boring and left it, but as he walked away the pangolin began to unroll itself, rustling the grass in the process and bringing the leopard back smartly. Again the pangolin rolled up and again the leopard quickly became bored and left it. When the leopard lay down a few metres off, the pangolin once more began to unroll, and so the whole process was repeated. We watched for half an hour or more as, time and again, the pangolin unrolled and the leopard investigated until eventually *we* became bored and left them to it.

This had provided us with a very good exhibition of the effectiveness of the pangolin's defence and on a number of subsequent occasions we were to see these interesting animals protect themselves successfully, particularly against lions.

Another means of protection used by the smaller mammals is downright aggression, an instance of which we saw one night in November 1986. As the mother and her cubs were resting in an open patch of grass near Big Dam, a genet came across the clearing towards them, quite unaware of their presence. A metre before it reached the leopards, the genet suddenly sensed them and stood up on its hind legs to peer over the long grass in their direction. The female cub was alert and leapt up and caught the genet. But the small animal wriggled and snarled and scratched with its paws, forcing the leopard to drop it. As the cub advanced on the genet again, it snarled aggressively, leaping forward to bite at her. The two circled each other for the next 15 minutes, the genet hissing and snarling and attacking constantly, the leopard striking with her paws and only now and then managing to bite it. Eventually the genet's injuries began to take their toll; its movements became more and more feeble until finally, fighting right to the end, it succumbed. It was a spirited defence and a less persistent leopard might have given up, but the tiny genet was no match for the big cat.

After that, the cubs began to make more substantial kills, the male killing a young waterbuck in November and the female dispatching an impala a few days later. Yet they still showed their youth and inexperience on occasion, the male once catching a young warthog and instead of killing it outright playing with it for about half an hour, running up into trees with it, dropping it to the ground, chasing it and catching it again, the hog all the while squealing loudly. It was only 20 minutes later that the piglet eventually died, more as a result of its wounds than through any conscious effort on the part of the leopard.

On another occasion the female cub caught and killed a female monkey. As she settled down to feed on it, there was a stirring in the grass nearby and a tiny monkey, presumably the dead monkey's baby, appeared. It crawled up to the leopard and tried to cling to the soft white fur on the cub's chest. Surprised at this, the leopard gently pushed the monkey back on to the ground with her front paw. But the monkey persisted and again stood up on its hind legs and clung on to the cub's fur for a few seconds before the leopard again gently pushed it back on to the ground. The monkey was obviously so young that it had not as yet properly imprinted on its mother and, now that she was dead, was choosing the nearest living object as a substitute. Had the leopard known what was happening we could have seen an unusual fostering take place. But this touching moment was shattered when the leopard picked up the baby monkey by the head, crushed its skull, and began to feed on it.

Two days later, the tables were turned. The female cub caught a banded mongoose between her front paws and was just going to pick it up when it bit her sharply on the foot, making her jump back and release her grip. The mongoose bounded away leaving a sheepish leopard licking her paw.

At the beginning of December 1986, 14 months after the cubs were born, the mother deserted them. At the end of December we suspected that she was pregnant once more and a few weeks later we saw her carrying a young cub between lairs. Less than a month had passed between the independence of her previous litter and the birth of the new cubs which meant that once again she must have mated while she was still caring for her young.

On the morning of 5 January 1987 we found the pug-marks of a female leopard with one cub on a road in the area of the Tugwaan to the south of the mother's territory. Hoping that they were the young female's tracks, Carlson and I returned to the area in the afternoon and, after searching for a while, found her lying in a thicket of scented thorn close to the road. We were able to confirm from her spot pattern that she was indeed the young female but at first there was no sign of a cub. It was only at dusk when the leopard got up and moved to the road, giving the cub call as she went, that we caught a glimpse of it. Obviously shy of the cars, the cub was running through the thickets after its mother but we were able to establish that it was a male.

We had further sightings of the young female on kills in January 1987 as well as brief views of the cub. As the months went by and we saw them more frequently, the cub gradually began to accept the presence of the vehicles until it seemed that he was becoming just as relaxed as the mother leopard's off-spring. This was the young female's third litter and it seemed that she was at last to have success in raising a cub.

In May 1987, when her cub was 10 months old, the young female gave us definite proof that leopards will actively teach their cubs to kill. Early one morning as we followed them along the bank of the Mshabene, we found both the female and her cub in a very playful mood. They chased each other through the bushes and up the trees, scampering around on the sturdy branches of a large leadwood growing alongside a brown ivory tree. After some minutes of this game, the female leapt easily out of the tree and lay down to rest in the shade below it, but for some time the cub scrambled about in the branches looking for the easiest way to the ground. Eventually he sprang down and joined his mother and together they continued to amble through the thickets along the bank of the Mshabene.

As they approached a particularly dense stand of scented thorn, the female spotted an adult female impala and, without any preliminaries, gave chase, catching it just as it tried to leap away. She held on to the kicking, bleating impala's hindquarters without attempting to kill it, obviously waiting for her offspring to arrive. As the cub leapt on to the impala the female leopard released her victim and it bounded away, shaking off the cub as it ran. Bewildered, the cub simply sat and watched as his meal disappeared into the woodland, but his mother reacted swiftly. She raced off after the impala, caught it and this time quickly dispatched it with a firm bite to the throat as if to say, 'Now this is how it's done.' Once the impala was dead, the cub returned, stalked it for a while, then leapt on to it and, just as his mother had done, bit it on the throat. We suspect that this behaviour plays an important role in the cub's learning process.

■   ■   ■

Over the years that we had been studying the leopards, their main threat had come from the other major predators – hyaena and lion – but in February 1987 they were subjected to a new, more insidious menace: disease.

An eight-month-old leopard cub carries a dead civet into a tree. Often mistaken for cats, civets in fact belong to the mongoose family and are omnivores which feed on insects and fruit as well as on small mammals. They are seldom killed by predators as a powerful scent released as a defence mechanism from an anal gland acts as a deterrent.

Fighting is another skill that will be required by leopards when they are older and need to assert themselves in defence of their territories. They learn this through play-fighting, an activity which is an imitation of the real thing. The two leopards stand up to each other, each striking at the other's face and neck with the paws and also attempting to bite one another.

Curiosity got the better of this young leopard which, on hearing a herd of 250 buffalo nearby, decided to stalk them. Somehow she managed to get into the middle of the herd before being detected. But the buffalo reacted aggressively, sending the leopard scampering up into a knobthorn tree, and then stood around under it for at least 20 minutes before moving off.

We first noticed something untoward when, close to the camp, we came across the female cub from the mother's recently independent litter walking slowly eastwards. She was in poor condition: the fur on her face was patchy and that on her body lacked the lustre of that of a healthy leopard. We assumed that this had resulted from the stress of adapting to life without the mother – an experience similar to Sticknyawo's – and we hoped that it would be only a matter of time before she pulled through the crisis. As we watched, the young leopard continued eastwards for a short distance and then rested in the long grass in a clearing. While she lay there, a kudu came along, stopping every now and then to browse off a bush and completely unaware of the leopard's presence. A normal healthy leopard with all the inquisitiveness of youth would immediately have reacted to the kudu and might even have stalked it, but the youngster did not even raise her head as the kudu passed her. We could see then that she was far from well.

When we came across her again towards the end of February she had killed a young waterbuck. Her skin condition, however, had greatly deteriorated. There were bare patches all over her body and red open wounds where she had repeatedly scratched herself. The fur around her face appeared grey and lifeless, contrasting strongly with the yellow eyes that stared with a vacant expression. We realized now that the leopard's condition was caused by something more serious than just a little stress, so we consulted Dr Roy Bengis, the state veterinarian in the Kruger National Park. After hearing our description of the symptoms, he told us without hesitation that the leopard was suffering from sarcoptic mange.

Mange is a disease caused by a mite that eats away at the skin, giving rise to an intensely irritating itch. An animal infected with mange loses most of its fur, scratches continually at the itch and in the process opens up wounds which become infected by bacteria. This secondary infection often causes the death of the animal. The disease is very easy to treat, even in wild animals, and the case that confronted us raised a question that we had often debated before: do we help the animal or not?

But in the first place, what had caused the mange? Roy explained that the mites occur in large numbers on the skin of most animals, living in balance with the host as long as the host itself remains healthy. However, as soon as an animal loses condition due to any form of environmental stress – lack of food during a dry winter was an example that he cited – the cortisone production in its body increases, suppressing the immune system and so allowing the mites to multiply, much to the detriment of the host.

We wondered what environmental stress the leopard was enduring. Obviously she was affected by her independence from the mother. For the first time, she had to find food for herself and, while she had already shown that she could kill successfully,

Lying on a sandy bushveld track, a female leopard
tolerantly allows her cub to play with her white-tipped tail.

previously she had had the mother leopard to fall back on. Now she was entirely on her own. Besides, it was obvious that there was a growing leopard population at Londolozi. Thus far, the mother alone had successfully introduced nine leopards into the reserve. Obviously other leopards living in the areas which surrounded her territory would also be producing offspring, so a time had to come when competition for space would begin to make demands on them. As Roy explained to us, it seemed that the disease was nature's way of controlling the leopard population. In addition, the leopard's main enemies, the lions and hyaenas, were also on the increase and as a result they were confronting one another more frequently. All in all, there were sufficient factors to convince us that the young female was under enormous stress, making it all the more difficult for us to decide what to do. By treating the leopard, we would not be relieving the stress factors in any way and might even be transferring them to another, more healthy leopard – the mother for example.

Over the next few weeks the leopard's condition deteriorated even further: she lost all the fur on her body and large bare pink patches developed where she persistently scratched. Lack of fur made her look like a long thin cheetah and if her situation had not been so tragic, her appearance would have seemed quite comical, for her tail was like a piece of wire and her thin neck supported an apparently enormous round head.

At this time we had a visit from a very good friend of Londolozi's, Tedd Schorman, an American who had been coming to the camp almost from its inception. He had never been able to bring his wife, Ellie, with him but had always returned home with photographs and stories of the leopards that made her increasingly envious of his visits. However, this year, he had brought Ellie to Londolozi for a few days and we looked forward to introducing her to her first wild African leopard.

However, the leopards were not co-operating and for four days we had no sightings whatsoever. Eventually, on the last day of the Schormans' visit, we found the female with mange near the camp. Having no alternative, we took Ellie out to see her. The leopard was no more than 100 metres from the camp and walking straight towards it. We followed, apologetically explaining to Ellie that not all our leopards looked like this one when, to our horror, we realized that she was heading straight for the rubbish dump. We could do nothing but follow as she climbed over the embankment into the dump and began to scratch around in it. She was a miserable sight and we found it most distressing that Ellie's first sighting of the usually proud and beautiful wild leopard should be of this hairless, mangy creature scratching about among the rubbish.

Fortunately, just before Ellie's flight was due to leave, one of the rangers found the mother leopard hunting along the

Pair of male waterbuck sparring.

Mshabene. We raced Ellie out there and gave her her first real sighting of a truly fine specimen.

While we were debating what should be done about the mange leopard, she moved on to the property of one of our neighbours. There, the ranger in charge quickly made a decision. He called up Roy and arranged for him to treat her.

Within a month she was looking better. Although her hair had not grown again, she was scratching less and there was an alertness in her eyes. As the weeks went by her condition gradually improved, her scratching stopped altogether and the red patches disappeared as the fur began to grow once more. By August 1987 she had fully recovered.

■ ■ ■

During this time, the mother leopard lost her new litter of cubs. We never discovered what happened to them but, after sighting them twice in February, in March we found the mother calling continually, obviously having lost them. This was the first litter that she had lost in eight years and it coincided with her daughter's attack of mange and the possible stress factors associated with the increase in the population of leopards and other predators. Was the loss of the litter no more than coincidence or could it be related to these factors?

At the end of March the mother was mating with an unidentified male. This coupling must have been infertile for in early April we again saw her mating, this time with the big leopard with the scarred face.

By now we had begun to build up some sort of picture of this male's movements and it seemed that he covered a much more extensive area than the 2 000 hectares of the mother's territory. Many sightings of him were made along the river and we suspected that his area extended beyond its further bank, but as we were unfortunately unable to go there we had no idea exactly how far he moved. A large number of unidentified males had been seen in the same area; he could have been among them although most of the sightings had definitely been of other leopards. Were these males merely passing through, or did they have territories that overlapped that of the scar-faced leopard?

Even more interesting was the fact that various different males had been seen mating with the mother. Sometimes she mated with the scar-faced male, on other occasions with some other leopard. Perhaps the mother's territory straddled the area where the territories of two male leopards overlapped. To answer our questions, we would have to find a male leopard tolerant of the Land Rovers, but this would be possible only if one of the mother's offspring, who had grown up with the vehicles, moved back into the area.

However, since we lost track of these young males soon after they became independent, we suspected that they were quickly pushed out of the territory by the dominant males. Possibly they would then try to set up territory in neighbouring areas, only to be pushed further out by other resident males until they finally settled down somewhere far removed from their home ground. There is a sound genetic reason for this: it reduces the chances that a male leopard will mate with his own mother. Altogether, it seemed that there was very little possibility that our questions would be answered.

Spotted hyaena cubs playing.

At the beginning of May 1987, we suspected that the mother leopard was pregnant once more. We found her on a number of occasions during the month scent-marking regularly and showing behaviour we had observed during her previous pregnancies. When and where, we asked ourselves, would she have her next litter of cubs? We knew that she had mated twice in a period of three months so we were not at all certain when the cubs would be born. If the first mating had been successful, they would arrive at the end of June, but if the second mating had produced the new litter, they would be born about the middle of July.

When June came around, we all began a careful study of the mother's movements. We would see tracks moving back and forth near one of her old lairs and someone would suggest that the cubs were definitely there. Then, two days later there would be more tracks going back and forth somewhere else causing us to hazard new guesses. Every one of us was eager to be the first to find the new cubs.

One day in June, after the mother leopard had been absent for some time, Carlson and I came across her while she was lying next to a pan. Her reaction to the vehicle seemed unusual. As we approached she lay low with her ears flat but after a few minutes she began to relax and when she stood up we saw that she was lactating heavily. We wondered whether she had already dropped her cubs and decided to follow her. She headed northwards from the pan through dense *Combretum* woodland and, after crossing the Mshabene, disappeared into a deep donga where there was an outcrop of granite boulders. For a long time we remained close by, listening, but heard nothing. When Carlson carefully checked the ground in the vicinity of the donga he found tracks of the mother going backwards and forwards to and from the boulders so we felt positive that it was there that the cubs were hidden.

We never knew for certain whether we were right for we did not see the mother again for nearly a month. When we did eventually come across her one morning in the middle of July 1987, she led us straight into a deep donga covered in dense dead brush. Obviously her teats were being utilized and although we heard nothing we were once again certain that the cubs were under the brush. That afternoon we followed the mother as she hunted in a large circle extending eastwards from the donga to Circuit Road Pan, then northwards, then westwards and south-wards again back towards the pan. Near it, she stalked a duiker and we left her resting about 100 metres from where we suspected the cubs to be. The next morning we followed her again as she stalked and chased a steenbuck before returning to the donga and disappearing into the brush.

During the night, she must have moved the cubs because the following morning we followed her tracks as she moved southwards from our airstrip into a donga about a kilometre from her previous lair. There, one of the rangers saw her curled up inside the pile of brush with at least one cub. Two days later, she had moved into a brush-pile 100 metres away in the same donga. We could hear the cubs calling from within and at long last had proof of the existence of the mother's seventh litter.

At the end of July 1987, the mother leopard again moved the cubs, this time to a pile of granite boulders in a donga just north of the Mshabene where she had previously had a lair. There we got our first really good view of two little cubs, no more than two months old, as they suckled from the mother.

She seemed to be choosing lairs that were ideal places for the cubs' safety for once she was inside with her litter it was usually quite impossible to see her. The crevice through which she entered the lair in the boulders seemed incredibly narrow and it was only with much manoeuvring of the Land Rovers that we could occasionally catch a glimpse of her cubs.

The importance of safe lairs was well illustrated to us in the middle of August after the mother had moved her cubs to a termite mound some distance from any donga or dense cover. To us, it did not seem a very safe place for there were holes in the mound big enough to allow a hyaena to enter. On the first occasion we visited the cubs in this lair, the mother was with them as they tumbled and played up and down the mound, but the following day we arrived to find no sign of them. However, as we waited, hoping that the cubs would show themselves, two hyaenas approached and began to sniff around at the openings to the holes. Apparently convinced that there was nothing inside them worth further investigation, they moved away from the mound towards a small marula tree, their tails curling up in excitement as they approached it. As one of the hyaenas poked its nose into a small opening at the base of the marula, we could hear the loud hissing of a frightened leopard cub. Only the tip of the hyaena's snout could fit through the opening and every now and then the cub must have scratched at the thrusting nose for the hyaena would jump back, startled. Then both hyaenas stuck their snouts into the opening and tried to dig at the ground, but the tree was stout and the cubs were safely ensconced inside it. After a few minutes the hyaenas lost interest and loped away.

When they had gone I drove the Land Rover up to the tree and bent over to look into the hollow. There, peering at me from the darkness, was the face of a snarling leopard cub. As I examined it, I wondered about the mother's choice of lair. Here, in the tree, was a little hollow of which we had not been aware, and yet it had saved the cubs' lives. The interesting question was: had the mother been aware of the hollow all along, or had the cubs found it on their own?

Whenever she realized that there were other predators about, the mother would become extremely cautious. One day at the end of August, we were following her and the cubs as they moved between lairs when she suddenly stopped to sniff the ground. She walked about in circles for some minutes, continuing to sniff carefully, and then abruptly turned around and walked back the way she had come. We looked at the place where she had been sniffing and found fresh lion tracks. Obviously sensing that they were nearby, the mother had turned back but, ironically, when she eventually settled down with the cubs in a lair in a donga, the lions were only 300 metres away.

Two days later the mother leopard killed an impala less than 100 metres from the lair. This was a perilous situation for the cubs for any predators attracted by the smell of the meat could pose a threat to them. That night the mother hoisted the kill into a large jackal-berry tree on the bank of the Mshabene and then moved up the donga to join her cubs. Once in the lair, she settled down to groom and suckle them.

The next morning, the rangers were out early to see how the mother had progressed during the night. Near the camp, Paddy picked up the tracks of a pride of lions which he followed southwards, past the airstrip and over the crest of land towards the Mshabene. There he found six lions, walking along the road parallel to the donga where the cubs had been left. When the lions were alongside the leopards' lair, they obviously picked up their scent for they suddenly turned at right-angles to the road and headed straight towards the donga. As they approached the lair, one of the lions, a young male, saw the leopard cubs on the ground and bounded off after them. One cub scampered into the protection of a pile of dead brush, but the other was less fortunate: the lion caught it just before it reached the safety of a tree. With a growl he bit into the cub, shook it several times, dropped it on to the ground and bit it again. By the time the other lions joined him, the cub was dead and they all took it in turns to pick it up and shake and bite it. They spent only a few minutes with the dead cub and then, scenting the more interesting impala kill, moved off in that direction.

The mother leopard was feeding on the carcass in the tree when the lions arrived and she immediately sprang down to the ground and ran off into the Mshabene. Meanwhile, two or three of the lions managed to climb along the large sloping trunk of the tree in which the kill was hoisted and began scrambling about in the branches as they fought over the meat. In a few minutes the impala had been completely devoured and the satisfied lions lay down in the sand of the Mshabene and groomed themselves.

It was only in the middle of the day that the mother leopard returned to the lair and found the cub's body lying where the lions had abandoned it. She knelt down in front of it, licked it gently and walked around for a few minutes before returning to it. Then she knelt down again and began to feed on her dead cub. An hour later she found the remaining cub and together they moved off, but for three days the mother continued calling for her missing offspring before leaving the area altogether.

At this period we had regular sightings of the young female and her cub. Invariably they were on kills within a fairly limited area between the Mshabene and the Tugwaan to the south-east of the mother's territory and both leopards were in perfect condition. Towards the end of September the young female deserted her cub in the area of the Dudley-Sparta Vlei and after a few weeks he moved away eastwards on his own to a neighbouring property. At long last the young female had successfully raised her first cub.

She was now well-established as a productive territorial leopard in her own area centring around the Tugwaan. We saw her again a month after the independence of her cub and were delighted to notice that she was lactating heavily.

The games that leopards play. Oblivious of the danger of precariously thin branches, a young male leopard chases after starlings in the top of a tree. Teasingly, the starlings simply fluttered from branch to branch, keeping just out of reach of the leopard and spurring him on.

LEFT: *Dwarf mongoose are inquisitive little animals that seek refuge in termite mounds and fallen hollow trees such as this one. Here a young male leopard tries to get at one.*
ABOVE: *Mongoose often respond to such intrusions by making high-pitched chirping alarm calls. Here the leopard reacts to the sound by cocking his head before making another attempt to get at the little animal.*

A young leopard tries to deal with a pangolin, an ant-eater covered in heavy scales and able to curl up into a ball for protection. Once rolled up, the pangolin remains quite still and the leopard soon loses interest. But as soon as it is left alone, the pangolin unrolls itself, rustling the grass in the process and bringing the inquisitive leopard hastening back.

Leopards will often tackle porcupines, but their sharp quills can pose a real danger. Once embedded in the leopard's paw or face, the quill can prove very difficult to remove. Quills can easily cause infection and even, in time, lead to the death of the leopard.

ABOVE: *Soft early morning sun catches a pair of year-old cubs play-fighting in the Mshabene,*
the main dry riverbed running through the centre of Londolozi and the core of the mother leopard's home range.
RIGHT: *His lithe body twisted into a beautiful S-curve and warmly lit by the early*
morning sun, a leopard sharpens his claws against the trunk of a knobthorn tree.

THE YOUNG MALE

In September 1987, the mother leopard, who was still concentrating her activities around the Mshabene in the vicinity of Three-streaked Donga, took her cub, a male, to a kill for the first time. It was a warthog that she had hoisted into a tree on top of a termite mound near Strip Road and this was the cub's first taste of a prey species in which he would come to specialize in the months ahead.

As he grew older, the cub's unique character began to reveal itself. Despite his traumatic experience with the lions, he had become extremely relaxed with the Land Rovers, more so than any other leopard that we had come across. Whenever we approached him, he would get up and walk towards the vehicles. Initially he would stop a few metres from us and stare inquisitively at various parts of the Land Rover, but he gradually became bolder and, provided we sat very still, eventually began to touch the vehicle, sniffing the bodywork, putting a paw on the fender and even attempting to bite the tyres.

The driver's door had been removed from all our Land Rovers and, sooner or later during his investigations, the leopard's probing face would appear only centimetres from a nervous ranger's leg. When a leopard is so close it looks enormous, even if it is only a few months old. Although the male cub did this kind of thing regularly, he was still very wary of any movement in the Land Rover, so all one had to do if he got too close for comfort was move and he would slink away.

On a hot clear day in December 1987 we found the cub resting on top of a termite mound where the mother had left him the night before. As usual, when the Land Rover approached he got up and came to investigate, sniffing at all his favourite spots. He sniffed the front fender, the front wheel and the bodywork near my legs. Then, suddenly and without warning, he disappeared underneath the vehicle. We waited for a while but he did not emerge on the other side as we had anticipated, but through a small gap in the floorboards I could see a small patch of his fur moving rhythmically with his breathing. Obviously the leopard was resting. It was a very hot day and he must have decided that this was the shadiest place to be.

It must be emphasized that although this cub and the others had become completely accustomed to the Land Rovers, they were by no means what one could call 'tame' – a term that we often heard people use to describe our leopards. They were wild animals in every sense of the word, free-ranging, hunting and killing for themselves and exposed to all the natural environmental factors to which, over thousands of years, leopards have been subjected. The only difference between our animals and leopards in other areas was that ours had never been chased or threatened in any way, so that they had come to accept the Land Rovers very much as part of their natural environment. At Londolozi, in fact, we had a rare example of man and a wild animal living side by side in some semblance of harmony.

Was it not a little dangerous to allow wild leopards so near to the Land Rovers? It was always the cubs who were the most relaxed, their natural inquisitiveness bringing them into close contact with us, and it was only as they matured that they would develop the unpredictable aggressive streak typical of leopards. Adult leopards were never as relaxed or as inquisitive and, until the cubs reached independence, it was reasonably safe to allow them to approach us closely.

But it was not only the Land Rovers that the cub stalked: he also enjoyed the challenge of big game animals. For instance, in December, when he was only five months old, we watched him stalking a group of giraffe that he had spotted while inquisitively investigating his surroundings. They were in a clearing, and he stalked them openly until they – being just as inquisitive as the

Three spots on either side of the face just above the whiskers help us to identify this leopard as the young male, born to the mother in June 1987. He became a real character, being more relaxed in the presence of the Land Rovers than any other leopard that we had come across and eventually grew up to become a specialist in catching warthogs.

leopard – all turned to face him, their ears pricked forward and their long necks craning. Whenever he came too close, they would turn away with a loud swish of their tails, lope off on their spindly legs for a few metres and then turn to face him again.

The cub's curiosity kept him very busy during the hours that his mother was away hunting, as we saw on a typical occasion in May. We came across him sitting on top of a termite mound staring alertly at the opening

Flame creeper (Combretum microphyllum).

stalk after them, sending them fluttering and calling back into the marula tree. This action did not deter our intrepid hunter who scampered after them into the tree and blithely ran about in the highest branches in a vain attempt to catch the starlings. The birds seemed to play along for, instead of flying away to the safety of another tree, they merely fluttered from branch to branch, remaining tantalizingly out of reach of the leopard but enticing him to follow.

of an old antbear burrow but as we arrived, he got up, sniffed around the entrance to the hole and then disappeared inside. After a few seconds small clouds of dust rose out of the hole and loud scuffling and high-pitched growls issued forth. We thought that the cub had caught something, but after some minutes he backed out of the hole empty-handed, shook the dust off himself and then tried to scrape sand away from the opening with his paws. He spent the next half hour or so trying every method he knew to force the cornered animal out of the burrow, but to no avail. We had no idea what was in the hole, but we guessed from the sounds we heard that it was either a mongoose or a civet.

Eventually, as the cub backed out of the burrow for the umpteenth time, he spotted an enormous male warthog which was heading straight towards him. Expertly using what little cover there was, the leopard stalked towards the hog until he was lying directly in its path. There he waited and, just as it crossed in front of him, he charged. Much to his surprise, instead of running away, the hog gave a loud aggressive-sounding grunt and charged at the leopard, forcing him to leap high into the air to avoid being impaled on a formidable pair of tusks. By the time the cub had recovered, the warthog was well on its way, running as fast as its little legs could carry it, its tail straight up in the air. The leopard bounded after it in a half-hearted manner and then abandoned the chase.

By this time, a white rhinoceros bull had ambled in to the clearing and to this the leopard turned his attention, stalking after it as it grazed slowly across the grass. There was no cover nearby, so the leopard simply followed the rhino in the open. Being short-sighted, the rhino became aware of the leopard only when he was a metre or two away and, reacting very quickly for an animal so large, swung around to face the danger. It advanced menacingly, sending the leopard running and then, having rid itself of the irritation, turned placidly back to its grazing.

Undaunted, the leopard, which seemed to be enjoying the game, returned to stalk after the rhino, climbing on to a fallen tree to get a better view. Again the rhino turned on the leopard and again the leopard ran off. However, as he stalked the rhino for the third time, a small flock of Burchell's starlings fluttered down from a nearby marula tree and began to feed on insects disturbed by the rhino as it moved through the grass. Of course the leopard found the birds irresistible; he changed direction to

Eventually, the starlings lost interest in the game and flew away and when we left the leopard was draped across one of the branches of the tree, fast asleep. He had had a busy morning!

■ ■ ■

During this time we were still getting regular sightings of the young female. She looked healthy and her pregnancy seemed to be progressing without any problems. We were not sure when the cubs were born, but on Christmas Day 1987 she led us to them for the first time. After my experience with her two years before, we had all learnt to be very wary of her and on this occasion we followed her carefully, keeping our distance as she approached a low ridge of granite rocks. A few metres from them, she began to give the cub call, repeating the low grunt every few seconds before leaping on to the top of the ridge and disappearing over the crest. From our position in the Land Rover we could not see anything, but we waited patiently until we heard the unmistakable high-pitched calls of the cubs as they made contact with their mother. We knew then that the young female had given birth to her fourth litter.

Less than a month later, she was mating again. We found her one night lying next to Mad Elephant Pan (named after an aggressive bull elephant that had repeatedly charged the Land Rovers for no apparent reason), with a large male leopard resting in the grass behind her. This was the first time we had seen this male and he was obviously very wary of the Land Rover. We watched as the female repeatedly got up and approached him with a low slinking run, rubbing her body against his face and then crouching down in front of him, the male responding with repeated low grunts. Her provocative behaviour persisted for at least half an hour and, although the male often got up and approached the crouching female, we did not see them actually mating that night. Because the male was so shy of the Land Rover, the pair kept moving away from us until we eventually lost them in the darkness behind the pan.

This was the second time we had seen a female demonstrating mating behaviour within a month of producing a litter of cubs and we were still no closer to knowing why this should be.

We obtained our first sighting of the young female's cub at the end of January 1988. She had killed a duiker in a patch of dense bush we called Princess Alice Bush and we found her only because an alert giraffe standing in the clearing had seen her disappear into the thicket moments before we arrived and was still staring at the spot. We followed up on this message and found the young female lying in the bush with the duiker wedged into a tree above her. On our approach, she climbed up to the kill, fed on it for a few minutes and then leapt down, giving a strange snuffling sound that we had never before heard from a leopard. In response, a small cub

Little bee-eater.

emerged from a nearby thicket to join her and we wondered if the strange noise was another method of calling young. We were to hear this snuffling sound on two further occasions, once when a young male leopard had been cornered in a tree by another leopard and once when the mother leopard temporarily lost her cub. We suspected therefore that it was some form of agitation.

As the young female was now spending most of her time in an area just off our property, our sightings of her became less frequent. It was only in March 1988 that we came across her again and on this occasion we found her, together with the cub, on a pair of kills, a duiker and an impala, that had been hoisted into two tamboti trees in the Mshabene close to Princess Alice Bush. We soon realized that both the female and her cub had mange. Black patches on their faces caused their eyes to stand out in contrast and the fur on their bodies was showing the symptomatic ruffled appearance.

That night, a hyaena arrived at the site of the kills. The cub fled into a tree but the young female stayed on the ground snarling aggressively. Eventually she charged at the hyaena and managed to bite it in the rump sending it, yelping loudly, into the darkness with its tail between its legs. Minutes later, two more hyaenas arrived, both with their tails curled up, a sign of excitement and aggression. This time the leopard leapt into a tree and stared down at them from the branches.

It was probably this kind of pressure that contributed to the leopards' contracting mange in the first place. We had not seen the young female for over a month and for all we knew she could have faced a threat of this kind several times during that period. Over the next four days, while the female and her cub were feeding off the kills, the hyaenas reappeared every night looking for scraps and harassing the leopards whenever they attempted to come down from the trees. As the days went by, the mange relentlessly worsened and this time, after much discussion, we consciously resolved to let nature take its course. Needless to say, we made our decision with extreme reluctance for we knew the leopard intimately. It had always been our policy to interfere as little as possible and despite intense argument among the rangers, the 'let nature be' faction won.

During May we saw the young female with her cub several times and on two occasions they were on impala kills. For a while it seemed that the mange was not becoming any worse, but at the end of May we noticed a definite deterioration. The young female was alone near the Dudley-Sparta Vlei when we found her. She was scratching continually and there were bare patches of pink skin all over her body. All the while she called continually for her cub which made us suspect that it had already died.

Then, on 10 June 1988, one of the rangers spotted a group of vultures circling above Gert's Clearing near Princess Alice Bush. He followed the birds until he eventually found them feeding off the remains of a leopard which had been dead for some days. The fur was in such a state of decay that it was impossible to make out any definite spot patterns but the ears were still intact and the left one had two parallel nicks in it. It was the young female leopard.

The 'should we interfere or leave it?' debate raged anew. By allowing the leopard to die from mange, were we not being inhumane, heartless, cruel? And what about the economic value of a leopard, such as the young female, who was completely habituated to the presence of vehicles? She could have provided our guests with years of excellent viewing of which, apart from the mother leopard, she alone was capable. The arguments were indeed very powerful.

But the counter-argument maintained that had man not interfered in the first place, the young female might never have died. By treating the first female to have contracted mange, pressure might possibly have been transferred to the young female. And if we had treated the young female as well, could not the mother have been next? And then, where would we draw the line? Would we continue to treat and protect every sick leopard that we came across, even if the population increased to such an extent that food and space became limited? Do we really have such a profound understanding of the workings of nature that we have a right to interfere with her control mechanisms on any occasion that might suit us?

The debate naturally led on to the broader issues of wildlife management. With the erection of fences across ancient migration routes, man has already interfered with nature to such an extent that some form of control is definitely necessary. Animal numbers have to be limited to prevent destruction of valuable grazing; bush encroachment, which was previously restricted by nature, now has to be controlled by man; and water has to be provided in many fenced-in areas where it no longer occurs naturally. While these and other forms of management are very necessary, the real challenge facing man today is to manage his wildlife areas with such sensitivity that he does not destroy what is left of the natural processes that produced these highly productive ecosystems in the first place.

The death of the young female was part of just one of those many processes. We had followed her from her birth six years before, and now she was lying in front of us, being consumed by vultures and maggots and already almost part of the earth. The maggots would be eaten by birds such as the francolin, and perhaps one day the francolin would provide a meal for a young leopard, completing one cycle and starting another.

■ ■ ■

We first became aware of the young male's imminent independence at the beginning of June 1988 when the mother leopard suddenly began to show unusual aggression towards him. They were together in the Mshabene one morning, lying some distance apart, when the cub got up and approached the mother as he had done countless times before. When he reached her, she suddenly snarled aggressively at him, struck him sharply two or three times with her forepaws and sent him tumbling to the ground where he lay snarling submissively. After a few seconds, he got up and again tried to approach her and again he was sharply rebuffed. He repeated his attempts two or three times and was roughly turned away each time. Eventually the young male retreated to the shade of a thicket and never again did we see the two leopards together.

The young male was about 12 months old when he became independent though this may have been a little early for within days of being deserted he had moved into the vicinity of the camp. We received reports from our staff that a leopard was stealing meat from their huts and that there had been many encounters with him.

However, every now and then the young male would make an excursion into the bush away from the camp. He would move in large circles through the surrounding countryside where he would come across more game and in this way build up his hunting experience. At times, we would find him stalking a herd of buffalo, sitting on the odd kill or just wandering about aimlessly. Once we came across him apparently resting on top of a termite mound, but as we approached him a family of warthogs burst out of a burrow inside it and rushed off with the leopard in hot pursuit. He must have caught hold of one of them, for there was a loud squeal and a cloud of dust rose into the air, but the hogs got away leaving the frustrated leopard vainly pursuing their scent in the grass.

On one of these excursions he made a determined effort to make contact with his mother. Late on a July afternoon in 1988 a ranger saw the mother leopard walking south-eastwards in the direction of the Mshabene, calling and scent-marking at intervals. Almost at the same time, the young male was found, not more than 500 metres away from the mother, also moving southwards towards the Mshabene. A Land Rover remained with each leopard to watch their progress. Whenever the mother called, the young male stopped and listened and then moved forward purposefully in the direction of the sound. The mother was calling with the repeated grunting call that we suspect the cycling female uses to make contact with males, and the young male was replying with this repeated grunt combined with the single grunt call given by cubs when they are making contact with their mother.

The mother leopard went on her way, ignoring the young male's calls. She crossed the Mshabene, drank at a waterhole on the south bank and then continued southwards. A few minutes later, the young male arrived at the same waterhole and drank. Now he had the mother's scent and he followed in her footsteps, responding to her call whenever she gave one. The sun set but we continued following the two leopards well into the night. At one stage the young male was no more than 100 metres from the mother, but, possibly intentionally, she managed to keep one step ahead of him. When we eventually left them, the mother had stopped calling and the male had lost track of her and was wandering about aimlessly, still calling continually. The next evening he was back at the camp.

We began to feel concerned, not so much for the leopard, but for the well-being of our staff, so we made numerous attempts to scare him off. Eventually, about a month after his independence, he began to spend more time away from the camp until he seemed to settle down in an area near the south-eastern boundary of our property.

■ ■ ■

In August 1988, the mother leopard produced her eighth litter of cubs. They were first heard in a donga covered in dead brush where she had previously given birth. Four days later we got a view of the two cubs in Three-streaked Donga, another lair that she had used before. She kept them there for about a week before moving them on to a place known as Warthog Skull Donga, after which we did not see them for several days.

Then, one evening we came across a pride of lions hunting to the south of Rhino Dam. They came up through a patch of thick bush and as they approached an open area they suddenly stopped and sniffed the air. We had seen them doing this several times during the hunt as the evening breeze drifted the smells of various prey animals towards them, but now, instead of stalking slowly in the direction of the smell, the lions broke into a run. They had obviously sensed something different for they moved so quickly that we had difficulty following them and keeping their ghostly shapes visible in the beams of our spotlights. As we bounced through the bush, Carlson spotted a pair of glowing red eyes in a tree ahead of the lions but just as he pointed them out to us, they came rapidly down from the branches and disappeared. They were the eyes of a leopard and into the tree it had hoisted the carcass of a duiker.

The lions, obviously hungry, milled around at the base of the tree, a tall marula with a vertical trunk, clawing at it in frustration and clumsily trying to leap up into the branches. To our surprise, one of the lionesses managed to get up into the fork where the kill was firmly wedged; within a few minutes the lioness had completely consumed it while the lions still on the ground became even more frustrated and hungry. Obviously, we realized, climbing a tree is not the safest way to escape lions.

After they had left the scene, we heard the leopard call just to the west of us and, following the sound, discovered the mother resting beside the road. She got up and began to move

Sitting on a fallen tree, a young leopard patiently waits for her mother to return from a hunt. As the cubs grow older, the mother spends more and more time away from them, only returning to take them to a kill or, if she has been unsuccessful, to move them to a new area before setting out on the hunt again.

northwards, eventually disappearing through some dense bush into the bottom of the donga where we heard her make contact with the cubs.

One afternoon in September, we received word from a wood-carver living about a kilometre from camp that a leopard had made a kill near his hut. We investigated and found the mother leopard on a freshly killed impala. She had finished feeding on it and, after grooming herself, stood up, stretched, yawned and began to walk southwards, scent-marking every few metres against a bush or tree trunk. Two days previously we had seen another leopard, the mother's daughter from a previous litter, walking and scent-marking intensively in the same area, and we noticed now that the mother was scent-marking in almost exactly the same spots. She spent a great deal of time smelling and investigating her daughter's scent, rubbing her face against trees and bushes and squirting copious amounts of urine on to them. Finally, satisfied that she had once again asserted herself, she moved out of the area just as it grew dark.

We watched as the mother leopard continued purposefully southwards. She crossed the main road, then spent a few minutes stalking a duiker which eventually saw her and ran away. Then she confronted a genet which sat on its hindlegs and stared inquisitively at her before scampering off. After travelling for about four kilometres – by which stage she was no more than 50 metres from her cubs – the mother came across a baby warthog that for some reason was not safely holed up in its burrow for the night.

Warthogs seem to be quite helpless in the dark and this one was no exception for it simply stood still as the leopard stalked it. We watched and waited in silence as the leopard slowly and carefully crept towards the unsuspecting hog. Cautious as ever, she made the final pounce only after 20 long minutes. The kill was quick: the hog made a brief squeal before being silenced and then the leopard quickly dragged the carcass to the edge of the woodland and hoisted it into a marula tree. She rested for a time at the base of the tree and then got up and disappeared into the donga to join her cubs.

The new litter remained in this donga for at least 16 days, the longest period that we had known the mother to keep cubs in one place. Our records up to then showed that she moved them every five days on average. This changing of lairs was very important as it prevented a build-up of smells and activity that could attract some of the many predators that posed a threat to the cubs. It was therefore unusual that she had kept them in this place for such a long time, particularly in view of the fact that she had a strong-smelling kill hanging in a tree which was no more than 50 metres away.

Fortunately, although there were a few hyaenas about, they did not prove a threat to the cubs who the mother was able to

This is a time of learning and discovery for a young leopard as he investigates everything in his surroundings. From experience, he will quickly learn that white rhinos are not to be stalked.

move successfully to a new lair 200 metres away. A week later she moved them yet again.

On 24 September 1988, for the first time the mother took her new cubs to a kill – an adult female impala that she had killed in a donga to the east of Big Dam. We watched as she fed on the carcass before eventually hoisting it into a weeping boer-bean tree on top of a termite mound. She rested in the branches next to it, groomed herself and then leapt down and went to drink at a pan a few metres away.

Two days later, we found the young male leopard lying in the shade of a thicket alongside Big Dam no more than 200 metres from where the mother and her cubs were resting beside the impala kill. When it grew dark, he rose and stalked a duiker that was approaching him across a clearing but when he was only about five metres away it saw him and ran off. Spotting a hare grazing quietly in the same clearing, he proceeded to stalk it, once again without success. Then, after drinking at Big Dam, he began hunting eastwards in the direction of the tree where the mother had left her kill.

When the young male was about 50 metres from the mother, a family of warthogs suddenly burst out of a termite mound beside him. Like lightning, he caught one of the baby hogs by the neck and tried to carry it away, but he had not grasped it sufficiently firmly and the piglet's loud squealing brought the mother hog running to its aid. Bravely she charged at the leopard, forcing him to drop the youngster to evade her. She turned and ran off and the piglet tried to follow but by then the leopard had recovered from the charge and once more leapt on to it. Again the piglet squealed, and again the mother hog returned and chased the leopard off. But the little warthog was by now badly injured and at the third attempt the leopard caught it easily. This time the mother hog did not return and the leopard was able to hold the piglet firmly by the throat. He dragged it, still alive and kicking, to the foot of a marula tree and there continued to asphyxiate it. The process took a long time, but eventually the hog died and the leopard was able to release his hold and sit up.

Suddenly he looked alertly past the Land Rovers and into the bush. Sitting there on the edge of the pool of light thrown by our spotlights was the mother leopard who had obviously heard the commotion and had come to investigate. The two leopards sat glaring at each other, the male snarling quietly, the mother just staring back. Eventually she lay down in a crouching position facing the male and watched as every so often he advanced towards her, snarling. After a few minutes the mother got up and moved back in the direction of her kill.

The young male then made an attempt to hoist the warthog into the marula tree. He managed to scramble up on to the first branch but, as he paused there to rest before making his next leap upwards, it broke and both the leopard and the kill came

Blue wildebeest at sunrise.

tumbling down. After that he began to feed off the warthog on the ground but when we returned the next morning we found him sitting proudly in the tree on top of the remains.

That afternoon the young male went down to Big Dam to drink and on his way there began to call. This was unusual behaviour for such a young leopard and it made us wonder if he was trying to locate his mother again. He arrived at the water's edge and started to drink, his pink tongue lapping at the water. His thirst quenched, the leopard stood up and walked up a steep bank at the back of the dam. As he reached the top his ears suddenly went back as he bared his teeth in a snarl and flattened his body against the ground. We could not see what he was staring at but almost immediately a large male leopard burst over the top of the bank and attacked the young male. The two leopards tumbled down towards the water in a blur of spots and fur but when they reached the bottom the young male somehow managed to slip out from beneath the bigger leopard. He disappeared into the bush leaving the large male standing beside the dam, looking from side to side. Suddenly realizing that he was surrounded by strange Land Rovers, the big leopard turned tail and followed in the direction of the younger male.

We lost track of both of them after that, but the following morning we found the young male back on his warthog kill in the tree apparently none the worse for his clash. The next morning he was still there but there was no sign of the kill which we suspected had been stolen from him by lions as their tracks were much in evidence.

As the leopard began to move slowly towards Big Dam, a family of kudu saw him and inquisitively began to follow him, their large oval ears pointed forwards. A game of cat and mouse ensued, with the leopard turning towards the kudu, stalking them carefully and then giving chase before turning away and allowing them to stalk him in turn. This was repeated two or three times before the kudu eventually ran down into the Mshabene. The leopard continued on his way to drink at the dam where we left him resting in the shade of a thicket.

During the course of the next two months we maintained regular contact with the young male but he was beginning to move further and further afield, covering large distances as he travelled. Every so often we would find him on a kill and, as most of them were warthogs, it seemed that for some reason he was specializing in them.

One night we found him earnestly following the scent of something in the grass. It meandered back and forth, the leopard following it in zigzag fashion for nearly an hour before the trail brought him to a burrow in the side of a termite mound. As he reached the opening, a family of warthogs emerged, but the leopard was right there, and he managed to catch one piglet which gave vent to a loud indignant squeal. This brought the mother hog running; she determinedly chased off the leopard, the piglet scampered down into the hole and the mother hog disappeared into the darkness. The leopard then settled down in a crouching position next to the opening of the burrow. Once he was disturbed by a hyaena and had to leap into a tree for safety, but he returned to his position and later that night managed to pull the injured hog out of the hole. It was interesting to see a leopard so determined to get one particular animal. It was the first time we had noticed some sort of favouritism in a leopard's choice of prey.

■   ■   ■

The mother meanwhile still centered her movements around the Mshabene and she and the cubs were not involved in any untoward incidents until two days after Christmas 1988.

On a cool drizzly morning one of the trackers, Richard Siwelo, was following a pride of lions along the Mshabene when he came across signs of a scuffle in the sand. As he studied the marks on the ground, trying to work out what had happened, he heard a branch move in a large leadwood tree on the riverbank. He looked up and saw the mother leopard sitting among the branches and feeding on something. Richard returned to the Land Rover where his ranger, Trevor Lindegger, was waiting with the guests. They drove through the bush to the tree and were shocked to find that the leopard was feeding on the carcass of one of her cubs. It seemed that lions had managed to kill it during the night and now the mother had hoisted it into a tree and was feeding on it, just as she had done on the two previous occasions.

She remained near the dead cub for two more days, feeding on it and calling regularly. Once, when the carcass had been half consumed, she carried it from the tree and made an attempt to bury it among leaves in the sand of the riverbed. Eventually she and the surviving cub left the area but four days were to pass before she stopped calling for the dead one.

We had been following the mother leopard for so long that we knew more about her movements than about those of any of the other leopards. As a result we naturally concentrated most of our observations on her, but we were seeing other leopards as well. A number of sightings were made of strange, shy leopards, including the large male with the scarred face, but more importantly, we were also obtaining increasingly frequent sightings of two of the mother's offspring, one female from her third litter, and another (the female who had contracted mange shortly after independence) from her fourth litter. They were now known to us as the Tugwaan female and the Sand River female respectively as both of them had established themselves in territories bordering on the mother's territory: the Sand River female along the Sand River to the north, and the Tugwaan female to the south in the same area that the young female had frequented. In the middle of September we saw the Sand River female together with

Alert kudu cow.

a shy male leopard and it appeared that they were mating.

Until then we had assumed that the territorial system in male and female leopards were similar and that any offspring would be pushed out of their natal area into neighbouring terrain by the mother and the territorial male. There they would come into contact with other territorial leopards which would force them off once again, until the young leopards would eventually establish themselves in vacant areas or defeat existing territorial leopards.

But the dispersal of the young female and now the Sand River female and the Tugwaan female suggested otherwise, as all these leopards had established territories immediately adjacent to the mother's. However, we lost track of the males shortly after they became independent, suggesting that the male dispersal patterns differed from those of the females. What few clashes we had seen between the mother and her offspring were not particularly aggressive, and this seemed to indicate a certain degree of tolerance between these related females.

Studies carried out on some of the other large African carnivores such as lion, spotted hyaena and brown hyaena show that they all live in social groups comprised mainly of closely related females with males dispersing from their natal area soon after reaching maturity. It is interesting to observe that, although the leopard is a solitary animal, this pattern of closely related females in one area still seems to exist, albeit in a more dispersed form than in the other more social carnivores. Without the aid of our identikit and the opportunity of following identified individual leopards from birth to maturity, we would never have uncovered this interesting aspect of the leopard's social life.

At the end of February 1989 one of the rangers sighted an adult female with a cub on Sunset Bend not far from where the young female had died. He was unable to identify her and we wondered if she could be the Tugwaan female with her first cub. In the middle of March we confirmed this by having a close look at this leopard's spot pattern when she was found with the cub on an impala kill in the donga of the Nyatini, a tributary of the Mshabene. A month later we were delighted to discover the Sand River female with a cub in the area to the north of the mother's territory. This meant that both of the mother's recent offspring had now produced cubs of their own.

Between April and July we had regular sightings of the Sand River female and her cub in the area to the north of the mother's territory and adjacent to the camp. Unfortunately the cubs of both females were very shy of the vehicles so we were unable to obtain any clear views. For four consecutive days at the end of August we saw the Sand River female, but without her cub, in the same vicinity next to the Sand River. She was calling regularly, giving a mix of the single-grunt cub call and the repeated sawing call and her behaviour was similar to the mother's when she had lost her cubs. Two days later, not far from where the Sand River female had been calling, we found the decomposing remains of a leopard cub. We suspected that it was hers.

■ ■ ■

In October 1989 we made another unique discovery. Early one morning, the trackers picked up the tracks of a pair of leopards, a male and a female, moving into the donga of the Nyatini. After following them for half an hour, they found the pair in a dense stand of young tamboti trees in the bottom of the donga. The leopards were mating but because of the denseness of the bush, the rangers were unable to distinguish any identifying marks on them. Then, after one bout of mating, the leopards moved into a more open area and the rangers were able to recognize the young male from the mother's seventh litter (the warthog specialist) born in 1987. He was just two-and-a-half years old and we were surprised that he should be mating at such an early age. What surprised us even more, however, was the identity of the female. She was the Tugwaan female, another of the mother's offspring, meaning that the two leopards were related as they had the same mother and possibly even the same father.

There were new questions to be answered. What had happened to the Tugwaan female's cub? Was it still alive? Then there was the question of inbreeding, which, in the wild, is usually prevented by the dispersal of the males from the home territory to areas far removed from their mother and sisters. In this case it seemed that the two siblings had found each other before that dispersal had taken place. Would the mating be fertile or was the male too young? If the mating did result in pregnancy, the cubs would be born towards the end of January 1990.

■ ■ ■

In the meantime the mother leopard had successfully raised her surviving cub. She deserted it when it was only 10 months old, much sooner than she had abandoned any of her previous cubs and we began to wonder whether this was a sign of her advancing age. We had first sighted the mother in 1979, almost exactly 10 years before. By then she already had a litter of cubs and, assuming this to be her first and knowing that leopards produce young from about three years of age, we calculated that she must be at least 13 years old. Could it be that with increasing age she was spending less time raising her cubs? Only time would tell.

ABOVE: *As one of her cubs watches with interest, the mother leopard drags a freshly killed duiker up into a tree.*
RIGHT: *Ears back, the young male leopard listens for the possible approach
of the mother warthog as he kills one of her youngsters with a bite to the throat.*
OVERLEAF: *In playful mood, a young leopard scampers about in the branches of a dead leadwood tree at dusk.*

Young leopards play in the trees with gay abandon, leaping into bushes unable to hold their weight,
running along branches that snap underneath them, and somehow falling to the ground without being injured.
Here a cub hangs from a branch, its full weight supported only by the claws of its front feet.

While the mother is away hunting, the cubs usually emerge from the lair in the early morning to play, chasing after one another and climbing up and down trees and bushes. Often, with the approach of the Land Rover, they stop their activity, creep down from the trees and disappear into a thicket for a few minutes before cautiously venturing out again.

LEFT AND ABOVE: *The young female, irritable from a severe attack of mange, snarls aggressively at the Land Rover just before her equally mange-ridden cub comes to greet her. Two months after this photograph was taken, both leopards had died from secondary infection resulting from the disease.*

A pair of giraffe in the dawn mist. Males are a full 50 cm taller than females and have horns that are both thicker and heavier. They fight for dominance by standing side by side and striking at each other's bodies using their heads. Males, like females, are born with tufts of hair on top of the horns, but these wear off as a result of fighting.

Most widely distributed of all the big cats, the leopard is found in a variety of habitats ranging from rocky hills, mountains and semi-desert to forest, woodland and savanna. An important habitat requirement is good cover and here a leopard takes advantage of long summer grasses to hide in as it rests early one morning.

EPILOGUE

In October 1989 the mother leopard produced her ninth litter of cubs. For days we observed her regularly moving about in the vicinity of the Mshabene. We could see that she was lactating and that her teats had been utilized but frustratingly she shook us off whenever she seemed to be heading back to the place where she had hidden the cubs. We visited all her old lair sites but found nothing until one day when John Varty had an experience that he will never forget.

Early one morning the rangers had found the mother moving away from a pile of granite boulders where she had left previous litters. In our search for the new cubs we had visited these rocks a number of times but without success. Deciding to check the place once more, John made sure that there was a Land Rover following the mother and that the ranger in it would radio him as soon as she seemed to be heading back towards the boulders. He did not want to be caught close to the cub if she returned. That would be asking for trouble.

John parked his Land Rover near the boulders, made sure his radio was turned up and, taking his camera with him, climbed down into the gully alongside the boulders to see if he could find anything. He walked around the boulders and, noticing a small gap beneath them, crouched down and peered inside. As his eyes became accustomed to the darkness he realized that he was staring into the face of a tiny leopard cub.

John kept absolutely still and watched as the cub slowly and clumsily waddled towards him. Suddenly remembering that he had his camera, he slowly moved his head until he had the cub visible in the viewfinder and began to film. Unbelievably, the tiny bundle of fur crept out from the safety of the crevice, brushed past the camera and stumbled along in the sand beside the rock. Then it turned around and waddled back towards John, its little round face bobbing up and down. Its large grey eyes

seemed to be misted and John's impression was that the cub could not see its surroundings clearly. It brushed past him once again and, to his amazement, tried to nuzzle into his arm. Then suddenly, as though realizing that this was a human being that it was snuggled against and that it was now in mortal danger, the cub bared its teeth in a snarl, hissed loudly, and tumbled back into the safety of the boulders. With heart thumping and hands shaking, John remained crouching in front of the crevice for what seemed a long time before he recovered his breath.

What had made the little cub venture from the safety of the lair? John suggested that it might have mistaken the sound of his feet on the sand for the returning mother and, still too young to see properly, it had set out to greet her and nuzzle up to her. Only when it picked up John's scent did it realize its error. John has had many exciting experiences with the leopards over the years, but for him this was the most memorable.

■ ■ ■

We have been following the mother for more than a decade now and in that time, due almost entirely to her wonderfully passive nature, our knowledge of leopards has increased from almost nothing to an intimacy far beyond any expectations. We have been able to observe first-hand nearly every aspect of their hitherto mysterious lives. We have watched the mother attempt to raise 16 cubs and we followed one of those cubs almost from the day she was born through the perilous days of independence, to the establishment of a territory and the production of her own cubs until she died six years later. And now there are two more of the mother's daughters at Londolozi, each with their own cubs that will no doubt yield further interesting knowledge.

Apparently oblivious of our presence, the leopards have revealed their hunting techniques to us, have let us observe their

The leopard is a master hunter, using stealth and its beautifully patterned coat to blend in with the shadows of its bush environment. Leopards will sit patiently like this waiting for a prey animal to make the wrong move. Only when they are almost 100 per cent certain of making the kill will they finally charge.

matings and have shown us how they interact with the other predators. We have seen the enormous threat that these predators pose to the leopard cubs and we have seen how the adult leopards contend with these dangers. They have shown us how they continually move their cubs from lair to lair, how they care for them, how they teach them to hunt and eventually how they desert them. We have seen how the cubs cope with independence, how they relate to other leopards after independence and how they eventually establish themselves as adults. And we have seen how leopards die.

Yellow pansy butterfly.

These remarkable discoveries would not have been possible without the amazing in-depth knowledge of the bush that the Shangaan trackers share with us. Their ability to find leopards is truly astonishing and difficult to explain in words. One has actually to be with them as they track to appreciate just how brilliant they are. The Kalahari Bushman has a reputation for good tracking, but I believe that even the most skilled would be given a good run for his money by people like Elmon Mhlongo, Kimbian Mnisi, Carlson Mathebula and Richard Siwelo.

Our Shangaan trackers were able to teach us a certain amount about their techniques: they could point out tracks on all kinds of surfaces and with some experience we learnt how to pick these out. They showed us the differences in shape between the tracks of individual leopards and also between those of a leopard stalking, walking and running. And they indicated the various subtleties of sound and smell that could help them detect their quarry. These observations depended on remarkable eyesight and hearing and with much practice some of us were able to match the trackers in these skills. But there was only so much that they could teach us for at a certain stage something else came into play. The trackers seem to have another sense, some natural wisdom that we Westerners lack, an intuition acquired from past generations whose lives had been intimately linked with nature. It is this wisdom that gives the trackers an inborn intellect to which we can only aspire. For a time it seemed that the talents of these remarkable men were being lost to us, but fortunately the development of game lodges such as Londolozi, which provide jobs for the trackers, means that they are still able to practise their age-old skills.

The rangers driving their Land Rovers in pursuit of the leopards have also played their part in this remarkable journey of discovery. Without their sensitivity the leopards might never have become accustomed to the presence of the vehicles. With guests paying to view the leopards, the rangers were always under pressure to provide the best possible views, but they never lost sight of the well-being of the animal, keeping their distance when it was necessary. The rangers' careful approach, especially in the early years, was one of the most important factors leading to the habituation of the mother leopard.

We have discovered much about the leopards but there is still a large gap in our knowledge. How exactly does the male leopard fit into the scheme of things? Compared with the number of sightings of females over the years, those of males have been few and far between. This is largely because there are no adult males apart from the mother's offspring that are really accustomed to the Land Rovers. But it could also be that male leopards occupy much larger territories than females and as a result are far more thinly distributed. Any assumptions about the males' status will remain just that until a relaxed leopard establishes himself on Londolozi. The possibilities of this happening are extremely remote as evidenced by recent sightings of the young male, born to the mother in 1987. At first it seemed that he had settled down along the Tugwaan in an area to the south of the mother's territory. But he didn't stay there for long, because two months later we received a report from one of the neighbouring game lodges that an unusually relaxed young male leopard had been seen and photographed some 15 kilometres south of the mother's territory. We compared these photographs to our identikit and were delighted to see that it was 'our' young male. This was a wonderful record to have as it was the furthest afield that we had ever recorded any of the mother's offspring and it was the first real evidence that males do indeed get pushed out further than females.

We seldom see the Tugwaan female as the greater part of her territory spreads on to the neighbouring property. However, every so often she makes an excursion on to the fringes of the mother's area and then we pick up her tracks or occasionally get a sighting of her. She seems to be a great deal less relaxed than she used to be and this is possibly because she no longer sees much of the vehicles. We are still not sure whether she succeeded in raising her cub although some of the rangers recently had brief sightings in her territory of a shy young male leopard that could possibly be her now-independent cub. We are also not certain whether the mating with her brother produced cubs. Even though she spends more time off our property than on it, we still keep a sharp lookout for her whenever we are in her area.

Recently, one of the rangers, Alistair Rainkin, while tracking with Carlson's brother, Willie, found a half-eaten impala carcass hanging in a tree only 100 metres from where the young female died. Together they searched the area intensively, but found no sign of the leopard responsible. After looking for it for an hour, they abandoned the search but I arrived at the tree only a few minutes after they left to find that the kill had been dragged away. The leopard must have been lurking somewhere nearby all the time, watching Alistair and Willie.

Together, Alistair, Willie and I followed the drag-mark into a dense thicket on the bank of the Mshabene. There we found the kill, but once again no sign of the leopard. We searched the bush intensively but still discovered nothing. Finally, we decided to park our Land Rovers a little way from the kill and sit there quietly and wait. Barely five minutes later, there was a sudden movement as the leopard leapt out of the grass, gave us a snarl and then grabbed the kill and dragged it away. We tried to follow, but the leopard was shy and, dropping the kill, she trotted into a dense thicket of *Acacia*. As she moved away, she gave a cub call a few times. We lost her in the thicket but we could still hear her calling every so often. Unfortunately we were unable to get a clear spot pattern but possibly the leopard was the Tugwaan female and perhaps her mating with the young male had produced cubs after all.

Saddlebilled stork in flight.

The Sand River female has given birth to another litter of cubs. She is now well established in an area to the north of the mother's territory and extending to the east and to the west of the camp. We have not seen her cubs as yet, but she is heavily in milk and her teats show obvious utilization. There is a network of gullies in her territory, including places where the mother has previously left cubs, all of which could make ideal lairs. We check these areas regularly and hope that it will not be long before we start having sightings of this new litter.

Thus both females seem to be well established in their territories on the periphery of the mother's, reinforcing our theory that all the females in a certain area are related. Strengthening the theory further is the knowledge that, since her independence in May 1989, the female cub from the mother's eighth litter has been moving around in a small area to the east of the mother's territory. Recently she was seen scent-marking, a sign of territorial intent. But she is only 18 months old and perhaps it is a little early to be certain that she is going to establish herself here.

This young leopard is another character that has provided us with much amusement. One of the rangers, James Marshall, describes one particularly amusing incident. 'Early one morning,' he tells us, 'we found the little female in a very playful mood in a *Combretum* woodland not far from camp. It had been raining during the night and large drops had collected on the leaves of the trees so that whenever the leopard leapt into one of them, the branches shook and a shower of water would descend. We were parked some distance away under a large marula and it was not long before the leopard began to show interest in the tree. She climbed up into it and rested on one of the branches on the far side from us. Then suddenly she got up and scampered along the branches directly above the Land Rover, shaking the leaves and drenching us all. It was almost as though she had played a prank on purpose.'

The Londolozi leopards are by no means circus animals or pets dependent on man, but wild creatures living their natural lives as they have done for thousands of years. They have no attachment to us apart from the fact that, after years of persecution, they have learnt to accept our intrusion into their world. There is, however, one sense in which they are indeed dependent on us for man has the power to destroy the animals and the habitat in which they live. Already, most of southern Africa's wild animals are restricted to protected areas, such as Londolozi, that altogether cover less than 10 per cent of the land. With sensitivity and foresight, man can ensure this small percentage is not, like the rest of the land, turned over to agriculture, industrialization or urbanization. While the economic value of wildlife is one of the most powerful arguments for ensuring its survival, there is undoubtedly a short-sightedness in this approach as it implies that unless something is of economic value it is not worth maintaining. As the human population continues growing, wildlife areas will become increasingly important – for their economic value certainly, but more significantly for their aesthetic value, as increasing numbers of urbanized people seek escape from their hectic world. It is this aesthetic value that man, as caretaker of the world's natural resources, must never allow himself to overlook.

And what of the future of the leopard in this broad scheme of things? In the past, with the Western world's strong demand for spotted skins, leopards were shot and trapped in their thousands, leading to a decline in their numbers and probably also increasing their elusiveness. More recently, with a ban in the trade of spotted skins in the United States and other Western countries, leopard populations all over Africa have been on the increase. The same can be said for the areas surrounding Londolozi where the leopard was intensively hunted in the late 1800s and early 1900s and where, apart from a few individuals that can be hunted by means of a permit system, it now enjoys protection.

Economically, the leopard can be a very valuable animal, providing a sought-after trophy for big game hunters willing to pay thousands of dollars to shoot it. While this destructive form of utilization may be repugnant to some people, it is worth looking at in some wildlife areas where leopard populations are increasing so rapidly that they are beginning to overflow from the protected reserves into neighbouring farmlands where they are invariably shot as pests. By utilizing for hunting purposes those individual leopards living near the boundaries of the game reserves, much-needed finance can be generated for injection back into worthwhile conservation projects – provided that the necessary tight controls are enforced. An added advantage of this kind of action would be the prevention of much of the antagonism that arises between the game reserves and their neighbours when the two forms of land-use come into conflict.

But the value of the living leopard is beyond dispute. Londolozi has now become famous for its leopards and people come from all over the world to see and photograph the animal that can be viewed with such ease in no other place on earth. The

word has spread that Londolozi is the place to observe leopards and for this specific purpose thousands of people have visited us, many of them again and again. This can be described as a non-destructive form of utilization and while the leopard can never be seen in total isolation from its environment, it certainly plays a large part in attracting visitors to Londolozi.

Ultimately though, man should see leopards not simply as money-making objects but as beautiful wild creatures perfectly adapted to their natural environment and living in balance with the thousands of other elements that make up the ecosystem. And it is on the adequate protection of this natural environment that the future of the leopard, like that of man and countless other living things on this planet, depends.

■　■　■

And what of the mother leopard? As I write, she is still alive, well, and about to leave a 17-month-old cub. She has shifted her territory westwards, possibly pressurized by her three daughters, although the centre of her activity is still the Mshabene.

She is old now and there is a feeling among the rangers and trackers that she doesn't have long to live. We hope when she does go that she doesn't just disappear, leaving us with another unsolved mystery. When she dies, it is certain that another leopard will fill the vacuum, but it is unlikely that there will ever be another leopard like her.

Very recently she had a narrow escape. As John Varty followed her one night, a lioness suddenly appeared out of the darkness and, with ears alert, trotted towards her. The leopard heard nothing until the lioness broke into a charge and leapt and John watched in horror as the two great cats tangled. Somehow the leopard managed to slip out from beneath those lethal claws and jaws and leapt up into a tree. What surprised John was how totally unaware the leopard had been of the approaching danger and we all began to wonder if her advancing age could be affecting her senses.

But the mother leopard is still with us and each day the game drives head off into the bush in search of her. Sometimes we lose track of her but, more often than not, the trackers find her in one of her old haunts, hunting or resting or sitting on a kill, and then we watch her and appreciate her gentle nature and feline beauty as she goes about her daily life totally oblivious of the impact she has had on our lives.

PREVIOUS PAGE: *Late afternoon sun throws long shadows over a leopard's body as it sits up after a catnap.*
ABOVE: *Leopards usually face forwards as they descend trees, running down the trunk rather than leaping into the air.*
RIGHT: *Aggression or something else? Glaring through summer grasses, a leopard pulls a flehmen face after scenting an area where another leopard had urinated. Leopards and other mammals grimace like this in order to activate an organ in the roof of the mouth used to interpret information being transmitted by the smell under investigation.*

The mother leopard nurses a pair of two-month-old cubs. Sights like this are rare as the female leopard can be extremely aggressive towards any intrusion and normally keeps her young well hidden. Cubs will continue suckling even after they begin to eat meat and will eventually be fully weaned at about four months of age.

In an unusual pose, a young leopard raises its front feet off the ground, the better to see over the long grass.

ABOVE: *With eyes glowing, a leopard looks down towards potential prey as darkness gathers. Although it has been described elsewhere, the leopards at Londolozi have not as yet been recorded leaping out of trees directly on to prey.*
RIGHT: *In a study of contrasting colours – golden-brown leopard's coat and black soil, pink tongue and dark water – a female leopard drinks from a waterhole.*

*Reminding us of the sort of views that we used to get, a leopard peeps over the edge of a termite mound
as it observes a herd of impala grazing nearby. Our earliest sightings of leopards, few and far between, were
always glimpses like this before the leopard turned tail and disappeared into the darkness.*

ABOVE: *Two youngsters peep inquisitively from the safety of their lair while their mother is away hunting.*
OVERLEAF: *Leopard cub siblings spend a great deal of time stalking and chasing one another – like these two caught in a blur of spots.*

THE MOTHER LEOPARD'S FAMILY TREE

Key
b. = born
i. = independent
d. = died
♂ = male
♀ = female

The mother, first seen September 1979
still being observed March 1991

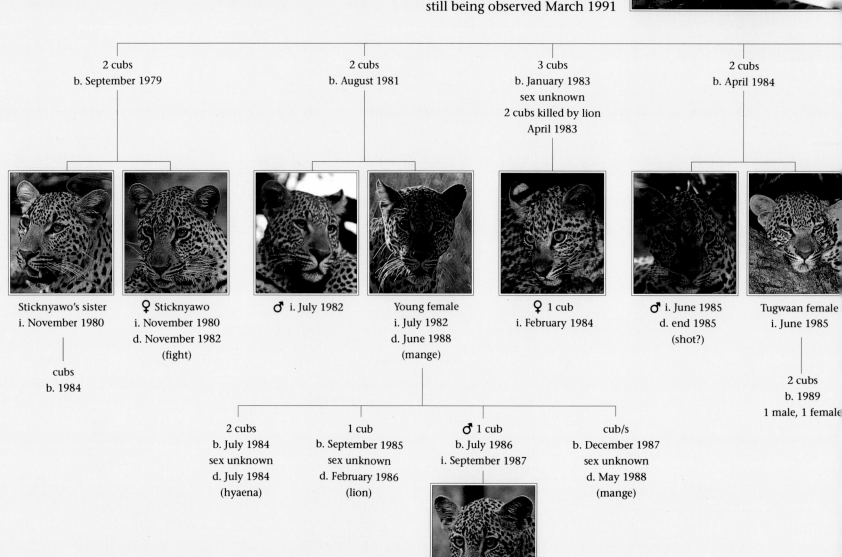

2 cubs	2 cubs	3 cubs	2 cubs
b. September 1979	b. August 1981	b. January 1983	b. April 1984
		sex unknown	
		2 cubs killed by lion	
		April 1983	

Sticknyawo's sister
i. November 1980

♀ Sticknyawo
i. November 1980
d. November 1982
(fight)

♂ i. July 1982

Young female
i. July 1982
d. June 1988
(mange)

♀ 1 cub
i. February 1984

♂ i. June 1985
d. end 1985
(shot?)

Tugwaan female
i. June 1985

cubs
b. 1984

2 cubs
b. 1989
1 male, 1 female

2 cubs
b. July 1984
sex unknown
d. July 1984
(hyaena)

1 cub
b. September 1985
sex unknown
d. February 1986
(lion)

♂ 1 cub
b. July 1986
i. September 1987

cub/s
b. December 1987
sex unknown
d. May 1988
(mange)

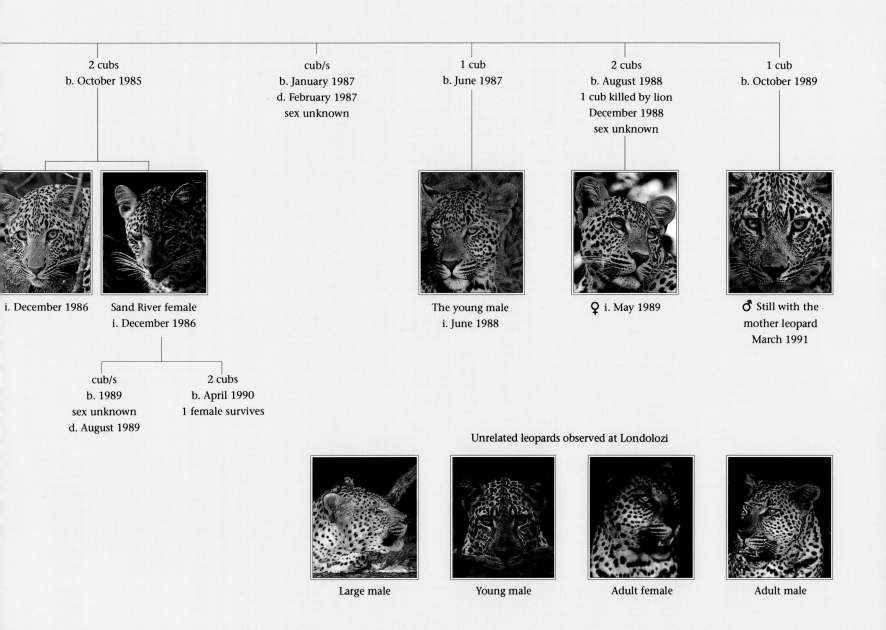

2 cubs
b. October 1985

cub/s
b. January 1987
d. February 1987
sex unknown

1 cub
b. June 1987

2 cubs
b. August 1988
1 cub killed by lion
December 1988
sex unknown

1 cub
b. October 1989

i. December 1986

Sand River female
i. December 1986

The young male
i. June 1988

♀ i. May 1989

♂ Still with the
mother leopard
March 1991

cub/s
b. 1989
sex unknown
d. August 1989

2 cubs
b. April 1990
1 female survives

Unrelated leopards observed at Londolozi

Large male

Young male

Adult female

Adult male

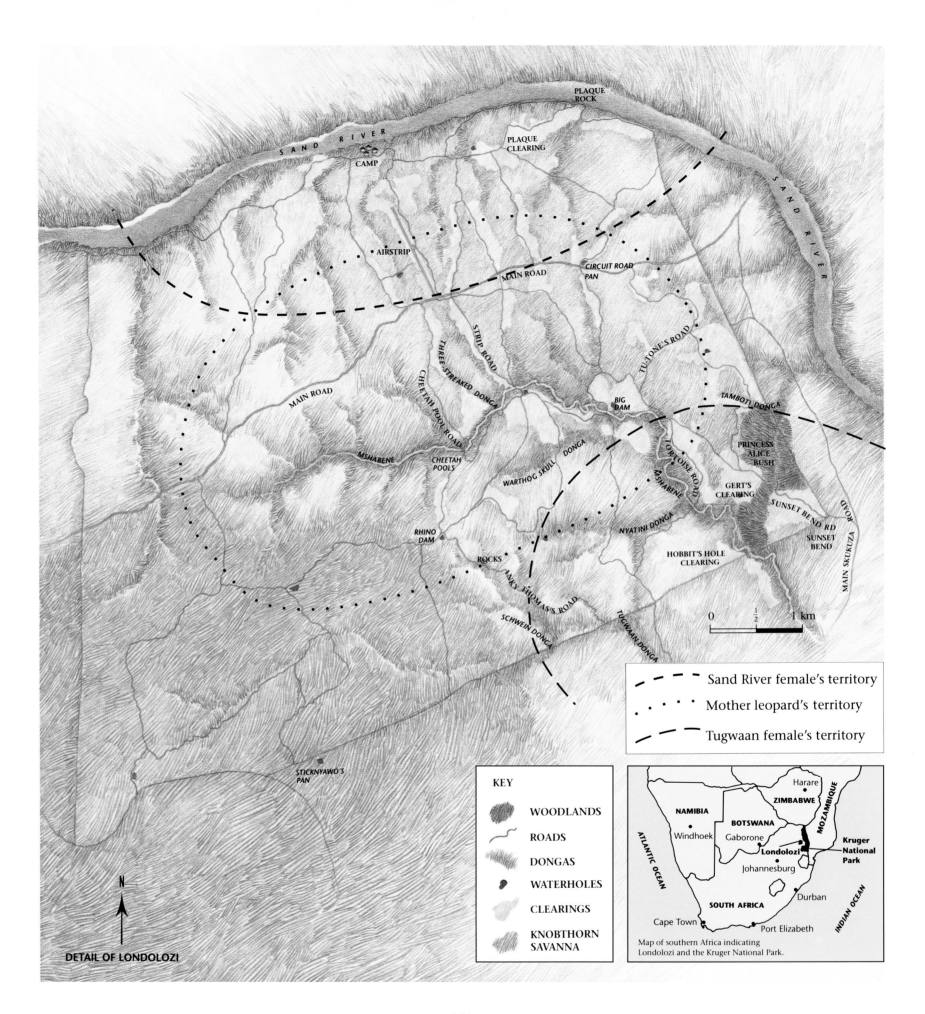

SAND RIVER

PLAQUE ROCK

PLAQUE CLEARING

CAMP

SAND RIVER

AIRSTRIP

CIRCUIT ROAD PAN

MAIN ROAD

MAIN ROAD

STRIP ROAD

THREE-STREAKED DONGA

CHEETAH POOL ROAD

TU-TONE'S ROAD

BIG DAM

TAMBOTI DONGA

PRINCESS ALICE BUSH

MSHABENE

CHEETAH POOLS

WARTHOG SKULL DONGA

TORTOISE ROAD

MSHABENE

GERT'S CLEARING

SUNSET BEND RD

GIYOR

RHINO DAM

NYATINI DONGA

HOBBIT'S HOLE CLEARING

SUNSET BEND

MAIN SKUKUZA

ROCKS

ANKY THOMAS'S ROAD

TUGWAAN DONGA

SCHWEIN DONGA

STICKNYAWO'S PAN

N

DETAIL OF LONDOLOZI

- - - Sand River female's territory

· · · Mother leopard's territory

- - Tugwaan female's territory

KEY

WOODLANDS

ROADS

DONGAS

WATERHOLES

CLEARINGS

KNOBTHORN SAVANNA

Map of southern Africa indicating Londolozi and the Kruger National Park.

NAMIBIA

ZIMBABWE

Harare

BOTSWANA

Windhoek

Gaborone

Londolozi

MOZAMBIQUE

Kruger National Park

Johannesburg

SOUTH AFRICA

ATLANTIC OCEAN

Durban

Cape Town

Port Elizabeth

INDIAN OCEAN

SUMMARY OF INFORMATION

The information summarized below is drawn largely from observations made on the leopards of Londolozi and may not necessarily apply to leopards from other areas which could behave differently.

Scientific name: *Panthera pardus* from the Greek word for leopard: 'panther'
English common name: Leopard
Afrikaans common name: Luiperd

Zulu name: Ingwe
Xhosa name: Ingwe
Shangaan name: Yingwe
Tswana name: Nkwe

DISTRIBUTION

The leopard has the widest distribution of any of the large cats, ranging from the southern tip of Africa over the entire African continent south of the Sahara, parts of the Middle East and spreading eastwards to the Far East, northwards to Siberia and southwards to Sri Lanka and Malaysia. While the question of subspecies is a controversial one, it is generally accepted that there are seven subspecies of leopard which have been separated on variations in coat colour and spot size.

1. Amur leopard *(P. p. orientalis)*: 10-15 individuals in eastern Siberia and an unknown number in Korea and north-eastern China. Endangered.
2. Barbary leopard *(P. p. panthera)*: it is possible that approximately 100 individuals still survive in the Atlas mountains of Morocco and Algeria in North Africa. Endangered.
3. Sinai leopard *(P. p. jarvis)*: found on the Sinai peninsula and in Israel. Endangered.
4. South Arabian leopard *(P. p. nimr)*: found in the mountainous regions along the Saudi Arabian Red Sea coast and the coasts of South Yemen and Oman. Endangered.
5. Zanzibar leopard *(P. p. adersi)*: a few individuals were once thought to occur on the island of Zanzibar off the East African coast, but this subspecies is now thought to be extinct.
6. North African leopard *(P. p. pardus)*: widespread over nearly all of Africa south of the Sahara and over the greater part of southern Asia including the Malayan peninsula and Java. In southern Africa found everywhere except for the Namib desert and the central Cape Province, the Orange Free State, southern Natal and southern Transvaal. Not threatened.
7. Anatolian leopard *(P. p. tulliana)*: a few individuals may still survive in the Caucasus and in Turkey. Endangered.

Outside national parks and game reserves, the last places where the leopards can be found are inpenetrable forests and inhospitable mountain habitat. However, the forested areas are gradually making way for human development and the only relatively safe areas for leopards are the rugged mountain areas where man is as yet unable to settle.

The rarer subspecies of leopards, such as the few individuals in Siberia, Turkey and Morocco, will survive only if their habitat becomes fully protected in the form of national parks or game reserves.

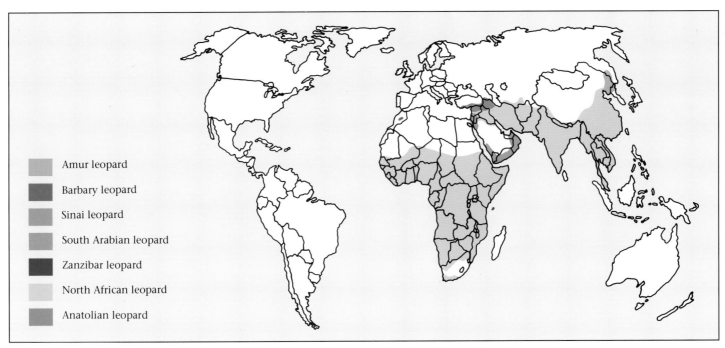

Legend:
- Amur leopard
- Barbary leopard
- Sinai leopard
- South Arabian leopard
- Zanzibar leopard
- North African leopard
- Anatolian leopard

Map showing world distribution of the seven subspecies of leopard (Panthera pardus).

DESCRIPTION

Generally a golden yellow base colour covered with a scattering of black spots arranged in rosettes. Rosettes become single spots on the head and legs. Stockier than cheetah and does not have that species' black tear-line from the eye to the corner of the mouth. The so-called 'black panther', often thought to be another species of cat, is in fact a melanistic form of the leopard which, through genetic mutation, is born with an all-black fur colour. Two normally spotted leopards can give birth to a litter of cubs with one spotted cub and the other completely black.

HABITAT

Wide range of habitats – rocky koppies, hills, mountains, forest, semi-desert, woodland and savanna. Generally favours areas with good cover. Found from sea-level to over 5 000 metres and in areas with a mean average rainfall of less than 100 millimetres to over 2 000 millimetres.

HABITS

Usually solitary except for a female with cubs or during mating. A male does occasionally join up amicably with a female and her offspring.

Predominantly nocturnal, but is far more active during the day than was previously thought. During the hotter parts of the day tends to rest in shady areas. Often rests on high vantage points, particularly termite mounds. Spends most of its time on the ground, but will climb trees to obtain a vantage point during the hunt, to escape danger or to feed on kills that have been hoisted. Will sometimes rest in trees. Young leopards spend more time than adults climbing trees.

VOCALIZATION

Has a number of different calls, the best known being the hoarse, repeated grunting that sounds like a saw cutting through wood. This call can last from one second to five seconds or longer and is used by females in oestrus or by both sexes to proclaim territory. Other sounds include a single soft grunt to make contact with cubs; a snuffling sound, which may indicate agitation; and growls and hissing when angry.

SPACE UTILIZATION

One male's territory seems to include the territories of two or three females. The female's territory is therefore smaller than that of the male. Territories tend to overlap and vary in size from 10 to nearly 60 square kilometres. At Londolozi the mother leopard's territory is approximately 20 square kilometres.

Territory is proclaimed by scent-marking and calling and if this fails, by physical combat. Males and females both appear to be territorial.

HUNTING AND FEEDING

The leopard appears to depend mainly on hearing and eyesight to detect prey. A stalker/pouncer, it uses available cover and infinite patience to get as close as possible before making a final rush. It catches prey with its front paws, claws extended, and kills with a bite to the throat, usually asphyxiating the animal. Sometimes a bite to the back of the neck proves fatal. Before it begins to eat, the leopard often plucks the fur off the skin; disembowelling takes place shortly after it begins to eat, when it starts at the soft underbelly between the hind legs. It opens up the carcass in this way and usually feeds mainly on the meat of the upper thighs. After a feed, the leopard will often cover the entrails and scraps with sand and grass, probably to hide the smell of the kill from scavengers. In areas where there is competition from other predators, it will hoist kills. It is not averse to scavenging.

PREY

The leopard is an opportunistic hunter and will in general take any prey that is available, the only limitation being the size of the prey. Mammals form the bulk of its diet but it also takes birds and reptiles. It often kills more than it immediately needs, but usually returns to these kills even if they are rotten.

At Londolozi 24 species of animals have been recorded as prey: impala, duiker and warthog comprised more than 77 per cent of all kills over a 7,5 year period. Sometimes individual leopards will specialize in certain prey, for example fish, bushpigs or warthogs.

Low down in the predator hierarchy, leopards have been witnessed forfeiting kills to hyaenas, lions and wild dogs.

REPRODUCTION

Leopards attain sexual maturity at about three years of age. At Londolozi, cubs were born in eight months of the year, so it appears that there is no peak period for breeding. Cubs are born after a gestation period of 100 days. A cub weighs 50 to 60 grams at birth, and its eyes open at 10 days.

The sex ratio of cubs born is approximately 1:1. Up to three cubs are born in a litter; the average litter size at Londolozi is 1,7.

Born in lairs among rocks, in brushpiles and in termite mound holes, the cubs are moved by their mother to new lairs every few days, initially by carrying. Cubs are first taken to meat at two months, are fully weaned at four months and make their first kills at approximately eight months. They stay with the mother for an average of slightly more than 12 months before she deserts them. The mean mortality of cubs before they reach independence is nearly 50 per cent, with most cubs being killed by lions.

COMPARISON BETWEEN THE THREE LARGE CATS OF AFRICA

This information has been collated from the references listed on page 167. The three cats vary in size over their ranges and because of this, weights and measurements vary greatly from author to author. For the purposes of this table I have generally taken the two extremes of measurements as recorded by these authors except when a particular measurement seems to be exceptionally different to the norm. In all three of the big cats, the male is larger than the female.

		Total length:		Shoulder height:		Mass:		Gestation:	Litter size:	Longevity:
		males	females	males	females	males	females			
LEOPARD	🐾	1,43 – 2,9 m		45 – 80 cm		20 – 90 kg	17 – 35 kg	Approx. 100 days	1 – 6 cubs	Up to 20 years
LION	🐾	3,2 – 4,3 m	3,0 – 3,7 m	120 cm	100 cm	150 – 240 kg	120 – 180 kg	105 days	1 – 5 cubs	15 – 20 years
CHEETAH	🐾	1,7 – 2,2 m		75 – 90 cm		35 – 65 kg		90 – 95 days	1 – 8 cubs	12 years

REFERENCES AND FURTHER READING

Ammann, K. and K. (1989) *The Hunters and the Hunted.* Camerapix, Nairobi.

Cillie, B. (1987) *Mammals of Southern Africa.* Frandsen Publishers, Johannesburg.

Grobler, H., Hall-Martin, A. and Walker, C. (1984) *Predators of Southern Africa.* Southern Books, Johannesburg.

Guggisberg, C.A.W. (1975) *Wild Cats of the World.* David and Charles, London.

Hamilton, P.H. (1981) *The movements of leopards in Tsavo National Park, Kenya, as determined by radio-tracking.* M.Sc. thesis, University of Nairobi.

Kruuk, H. (1972) *The Spotted Hyaena: a study of predation and social behavior.* University of Chicago Press, Chicago.

Le Roux, P. (1984) *The ecology of the leopard in the Londolozi Game Reserve.* Unpublished B.Sc. Honours thesis, University of Pretoria, Pretoria.

Le Roux, P. and Skinner, J. (1989) A note on the ecology of the leopard in the Londolozi Game Reserve, South Africa. *African Journal of Ecology*, Volume 27, pp. 167-171.

MacDonald, D. (ed.) (1984) *The Encyclopedia of Mammals:1.* George Allen and Unwin, London.

Moss, C. (1976) *Portraits in the Wild.* Hamish Hamilton, London.

Schaller, G.B. (1972) *The Serengeti Lion: a study of predator-prey relations.* University of Chicago Press, Chicago.

Scott, J. (1985) *The Leopard's Tale.* Elm Tree Books/Hamish Hamilton, London.

Smithers, R.H.N. (2nd ed. 1990) *The Mammals of the Southern African Subregion.* University of Pretoria, Pretoria.

Stuart, C. and T. (1990) *Field Guide to the Mammals of Southern Africa.* Struik Publishers, Cape Town.

Turnbull-Kemp, P. (1967) *The Leopard.* Howard Timmins, Cape Town.

Von Lawick, H. (1977) *Savage Paradise.* Collins, London.

Walker, C. (1988) *Signs of the Wild.* Struik Publishers, Cape Town.

Wolhuter, H. (1948) *Memories of a game ranger.* The Wildlife Protection Society of Southern Africa.

INDEX

LIST OF SUBSCRIBERS

SPONSORS' EDITION

Stephen Bales

Mr and Mrs F.J. Barrell

Jim Gerard Paul Broekhuysen

P. Campbell

The Rt Hon. Viscount Chetwynd

Dr H.B. Dyer

Patrick, Kathryn, Gayle, Sally and Bradley Flanagan

R.W. Hancock

Lydia Gorvy

Geoff and Joan Robin

Struik Winchester

The Hes family

Dr H.G. van Heerden

D.B. Varty

John Varty

M. Varty

Dr W.P. Venter

Phillip John Wharton

COLLECTORS' EDITION

Ian Alexander
Mackey Arnstein
Geoff and Mary Ash
Bob Barlow
Alex A. Barrell
Eberhard Bertelsmann
Bevan family
David K. Bond
Sarah, Caroline and Simon Borchert
B. Braude
Pat and Mike Buchel
Dr F.R. Callige
Nigel and Vicki Colne
Prof. J.L. Couper
Jennifer Crisp
David Cruse
Donald and Rosemary Curri
Ray Deeley
W.R. Doepel and R.A. Sharkin
Chloe Droste
A.M. Dyer and J. O' Regan
Dr H.B. Dyer
John Fannin
Clive and Lynda Fisher
Stephen Fitzgerald
Malcolm Foster

Russel, Bonnie and Gabriella Friedman
Nucha Goncalves
Steven Hall
Rolf Willy Hansen and Ingeborg Sundet
John K. Hepburn
Keith Hepburn
Basil Hersov
Dave and Margie Hidden
R.W.B. Hodgson
Rupert Horley
F.W. Hosken
Hunt Leuchars and Hepburn Holdings Ltd
Ismail Hussain
Mike and Leigh Kay
M.F. Keeley
Keith Krog
Micheline Logan
Desmond Lund
Helen MacGregor
O.J. Mackenzie
Kelly Manson
Ian McCall
Michael Charles Mullins
Jan and Elizabeth Nel
N.J. North
Danie, Nita, Daniel and Christiaan Olivier

Kiki Pashiou
John and Jeannine Pearse
Neil and Toni Ponting
Helmut and Pamela Redtenbacher
Brenda and Wim Reinders
Rodney K. Reynolds
John Rundle
Jennifer M. Shadrach
Cyril David Shaw
H.P. St Quintin
Paul A. Stone
Pieter Struik
Struik Winchester
B.J. Swart
The Brenthurst Library
Ian R.F. Trollip
G.A. Upfill-Brown
Arsene van den Driessche
W. van Rÿswÿck
Dr H.J. van Wyk
Dr Hans Walker
Roy and Lorraine Webber
Edmund H. White
Peter and Jeffe Williams
Heather Zietsman

STANDARD EDITION

Catherine M. Abrey
Dérell and Anthony Adams
P.D. Adams
Willi Aerne
Africana Book Collectors
Bronwyn Allan
Margaret J.D. Anderson
Mark and Celia Andrews
Bill and Charlotte Armstrong
M.L. Arnold
Eric M. Arnot
Shelly Aronson
Brian Askew
J.P.E. Atherton
A.E. Bailey
Michaela Baker
Gina Baldo
Sharna Balfour
Paul Bannister

N.E.C. Barlow
Thomas Barlow
David Barnes
M.R. Barnes
Mr and Mrs C. Barrow
Mary Barton
A.A.J. Bastenie
Kim Louise Bauer
Mr and Mrs E.R. Bebington
Reinher Behrens
Patricia Bellingan
Roland Bellstedt
Graham Benfield
C.H. Berman
Birch Bernstein
Prof. Gerhard J. Beukes
Mr and Mrs W.F.L. Blanden
Central Bookshop Ltd, Blantyre
Mr and Mrs Bloch

Verena Boehm
M. Botero
C.J.Z. Bourhill
A.E. and J.M. Bowland
Leslie and Sheena Boyd
Chris Bradley
Alison Brand
Wendy Branson
Peter Brigg
Anthony J. Broekhuizen
E.A. Brönn
Ray and Margo Brough
Carl Bruessow
Max Bruessow
Neville and Barbara Bucke
L.R. Burchell
R.G. Burkhalter
Veronica Burzelman
M.D. Butler

Chris and Elsie Calitz
D. and R. Carbutt
Neil and Val Card
Mr and Mrs R.G. Cathcart-Kay
P.S.M. Cawthorn
John Chappell
Carol and Saj Chaudry
Bernard and Jill Chipkin
N.D. Christie
C.J. Cilliers
Johann and Steph Coetzee
John and Dee Collard
Jean Collier
C. Leonard Collins
Leon Conradie
Elisabeth Cooper
Marie and Peter Copland
Pietro Corgatelli
Dr Graham Coupland

A.B. Cowden
Michael Leonard Craig
Harold H. Currie
Dennis, Jenny, Mandy
  and Richard Da Silva
Samuel Crown Dansie
Joyce Davidson
Marcus Davidson
Andrea and Candice Davison
Francie de Klerk
Hilary de Kok
Leon and Carine de Lange
Dr Johan de Wet
Dave Delbridge
I.G. Dennler
Kevin Deutschmann
John and Sara Dewar
Mrs Angela Dickinson
Geoffrey and Shirley Dicks
Klaus Dienst
Roy Dinsdale
David Colin Dix
Louisa Doble
Leon and Ronel Drotsky
I.M. McK Drummond
I.W. du Preez
Malan du Preez
Dr Francois du Randt
Claude Ducommun
Jon Eagar
Rob and Trudi Earle
Fritz Eckl
Gary Ronayne Edwards
Mike and Janine Egan
Trevor and Maria Elliot
Peter Ellis
Roger and Sue Ellis
R.R. Emmett
Hans C. Ernst
L.P. Evans
Vincent Faris
Gavin Faulds
Luke Fiske
David and Elaine Forbes
Margaret Fordyce
John and Christine Foreman
Suzanne Fortescue
Dorothy Foster
Malcolm Foster
Beverley Fourie
David Fridjhon

Willem P. Frost
Gianni and Rensche Galetti
R.E Garratt
Michael Georgiou
U. Gericke
Tony and Shane Girling
David and Joan Gladding
B.M. Glyn
Liz and Mark Going
Mel Goott
David Gordon
Dr M.C. Gordon Grant
V. Gore
Beryl Gosling
Mary and Margaret Grafton
D.A. Gray
Adin and Sharon Greaves
M.V. Greene
Julie Greensmith
Robert Griffin
Siegfried Gross
J.C. Grundy
Clifford David Gundry
P.H. Gutsche
HL and H Timber
  Holdings (Pty) Ltd
Anthony, Bernie, Andre and
  Tony Hall
Jean and Eric Hall
Leonard Hall
Rudolf Hanni
G.C. Harris
Prof. Paddy Harrison
Peter Harrison
Tony and Vicky Harrison
R.E. Hassler
Fraser Hastings
John M. Hayes
Ian Head
Colin Heath
Ernest Helm
Rex and Coral Hendy
Ashleigh Morgan Henning
Basil Hersov
Jim Hes
Karen and Neil Hes
Dave and Margie Hidden
L.S. Hill
D.A. Hilton Barber
R.D. Hirst
Patricia Hobday

R.L. Holing
A.J.M. Holmes
Diana Hood
Barbara and Owen Hooker
Ingrid Sophie Horsch
Errol Hotz
Liz and Arnd Huesmann
Neil Hulett
B.J.E. Human
Heike Hundsdörfer
Graham Hunt
Lindsay Hunt
Roland Hunt
Jenny and Ted Hurworth
Julian Bryan Hutchins
Jane Hutson
Clive Scott Johnson
Jan Jack
Edwin Jacobs
Harold and Kiki Jackson
Adriaan and Jenny Jacobsz
R.J.F. James
Jean Pierre Jannette Walen
J.K. Jasper
Andrew and Barbi Jay
Christine Jeffrey
Lavinia and Derek Jelley
Elaine Anne Jones
Robert A. Kadur
Wayne Kahn
B.A. Kantey
Jeremy Kilian
Leslie S. King
Keith and Kim Kirby
Michael Kirkinis
Keith Edward Kirsten
Kishoo
Timothy Luke Klapwijk
D. Klein
D.G. Knott
Ilona and Ruth Kolbé
André and Ronél Koorts
Neil Krawitz
Rodney W. Kretschmar
Errol and Freda Kreutzer
Lucille Krige
Peter Paul Krog
Yvonne Kruger
Ofer Kubbi
A.W. Kuhn
Eric and Isobyl La Croix

Johan Latsky
Mr and Mrs P.J. Lavies
Kate Law
R.M. Lawrie
L.E. Leach
C.D. Lear
Ms K.E. Lear-Christoffersen
John Lee
Joan Lemmer
John Lennard
Pete and Jane le Roux
Letaba Arts and Crafts
Allan H. Levin
Elizabeth Jones Levitz
Ilana Levy
Ian D. Lewis
Lex Hollman Trust
Mr and Mrs A.J.M. Lind
Ian Hamilton Little
Lynton and Iris Lockwood-Hall
A.C. Logie
Piet Lombard
Athol Loppnow
Joe Louw
At and Julene Lubbe
Shelagh Mary Lubbock
Lionel Lucas
Clive and Wendy Lucas-Bull
F.P. Lucks
T. Ludin
Ann Magnus
J. Maidsmith
Ari Yoel Mandelberg
Andre and Ann Marais
Ann and Bill Marklew
Andrew M. Marthinusen
R. Massey-Hicks
Mark Matheson
Neville and Cynthia Matterson
Mbulwa Estate Limited
Eric and Nola McCabe
Brian and Sally McCormick
S.B. McDermott
Bruce W. McDonald
Peter O. McDougall
Dr A.D.G. McGregor
Jane and Martin Mealin
Maurice Jack Robert Meano
Joan and Mick Melle
Miriam Meltzer
S. Metzer